Analysis of means in some non-standard situations

J.B. Dijkstra

Centrum voor Wiskunde en Informatica
Centre for Mathematics and Computer Science

1980 Mathematics Subject Classification: 62F35.
ISBN 90 6196 347 8
NUGI-code: 811

Preface

CB-Stk = Math
SciMON Sep

This is a study on methods for comparing several mean values when the assumptions for a classical test are not fulfilled.

For normal distributions with unequal and unknown population variances some tests for the hypothesis of equal location parameters are compared. Besides some methods that are specially designed for this situation some attention is also given to the robustness of the Kruskal and Wallis test against variance heterogeneity.

For symmetric distributions two nonparametric methods are considered that adapt themselves to the estimated tail-weights. It is demonstrated that these tests have more power than some non-adaptive tests for a representative mixture of distributions.

Several approaches are considered for dealing with the possible occurrence of some extreme outliers. This is done for normal distributions and equal variances. Outliers are represented by symmetric and one-sided contamination.

For almost every well known classical Multiple Comparisons Test alternatives are given that can deal with variance heterogeneity or with some extreme outliers. These modifications are compared and some recommendations are given.

Several people have contributed to this study and I want to express my gratitude to them. In alphabetical order they are: Prof. dr. W. Albers, Prof. dr. R. Doornbos, J. Hontelez, J.C. Linders, Ir. L. van Reij, R.V.H. Rooijakkers, Prof. dr. P.J. Rousseeuw, Prof. dr. P.C. Sander, T. Smeulders, Mrs. E.H.A.M. Stijnen-Stribos and Ir. P.S.P.J. Werter.

Table of Contents

1. Introduction

This tract is about the hypothesis that some location parameters are equal. The model is:

$$x_{ij} \simeq \mu_i + e_{ij}$$

The chapters number 2, 3, 4 and 5 consider the hypothesis H_0: $\mu_1 = ...$ $= \mu_k$ where the observations within the samples are numbered from 1 to n_i. Chapter 6 is about a collection of hypotheses: $\mu_i = \mu_j$, where i = 1 , ... , k and j = 1 , ... , i-1. For the errors e_{ij} various distributions will be considered with $Ee_{ij} = 0$ and special attention will be given to normal distributions with variance heterogeneity and to the presence of some extreme outliers.

As a consequence of several approximations the probability of rejecting a hypothesis when in fact it is true will not for every test be equal to the chosen size α. In those situations methods are considered for which this probability differs as little as possible from α, whatever the value of the nuisance parameters may be. For example, in the Behrens–Fisher problem there are two samples from normal distributions with unknown and possibly different variances. The nuisance parameter here is θ, the ratio of the population variances. Following the Neyman and Pearson conditions a validation of a test for which the distribution under the hypothesis is only approximately known, involves repeated sampling for fixed θ. For every value of θ the fraction of samples for which the hypothesis is rejected under H_0 should be almost equal to α. When no analytical approach seems to exist a simulation is performed with a limited set of values for θ that should represent the collection one might meet in practical situations.

Those who are in favour of fiducial statistics see the ratio θ^* of the sample variances as the nuisance parameter in the Behrens–Fisher problem. And they are lucky, because there exists an exact solution for this problem. This is usually called the Behrens–Fisher test [Behrens (1929), Fisher (1935)] and for every fixed value of θ^* the probability of rejecting a true hypotheses is α. But that is not the case for every fixed value of θ. Only for $\theta = 0$ or $\theta = \infty$ the Behrens–Fisher test controls the confidence error probability. For all other values of θ this method is conservative in the classical sense [Wallace (1980)]. In this study conservatism will be regarded as undesirable, because it usually results in a loss of power. Progressiveness (meaning that the actual level exceeds its nominal value) is considered to be unacceptable.

The Behrens-Fisher solution uses the following distribution:

$$\frac{\mu_1-\mu_2-(x_1-x_2)}{\sqrt{s_1^2/n_1+s_2^2/n_2}} \simeq BF(\nu_1,\nu_2,\theta^*)$$

Here x_i denotes the sample mean and s_i^2 the sample variance. The tables are entered with the numbers of degrees of freedom $\nu_i = n_i-1$ and the ratio θ^*. In the original publication the following parameter was used instead of θ^* :

$$\theta^{BF} = \sin^{-1}\sqrt{(s_1^2/n_1)/(s_1^2/n_1+s_1^2/n_2)}$$

The desideratum of all tests in this dissertation is that the nominal level α controls the error probability under the hypothesis. This probability is considered with the classical confidence meaning. Therefore the fiducial solutions will be discarded and for the Behrens-Fisher problem approximate solutions like Welch's (1947) modified t-test will be recommended.

1.1. Variance heterogeneity

Chapter 2 is about tests for the equality of several means when the population variances are unequal. The data are supposed to be normally and independently distributed. The situation can be described as the k-sample Behrens-Fisher problem, and several approximate solutions are considered. In order to understand why such special tests are necessary it is of interest to know what will happen if the classical method is used and the problem of variance heterogeneity is simply ignored. Table 1 gives the estimated size of the classical test for one-way analysis of variance. For the nominal size the usual values of 10%, 5% and 1% were chosen. The statistic F is given by:

Table 1: Actual size of classical F-test				
sample size	sigma	10%	5%	1%
4,6,8,10,12	1,1,1,2,2	6.28	3.16	0.72
	1,1,2,3,3	5.88	3.12	0.72
	1,2,3,4,5	5.52	2.72	0.56
	1,2,3,5,7	5.92	2.88	0.76
	2,2,1,1,1	22.28	14.20	6.04
	3,3,2,1,1	26.00	17.64	8.08
	5,4,3,2,1	27.12	19.52	9.24
	7,5,3,2,1	31.28	24.44	13.28
8,8,8,8,8	1,1,1,2,2	11.72	6.92	1.88
	1,1,2,3,3	12.00	7.08	2.32
	1,2,3,4,5	12.60	7.88	2.24
	1,2,3,5,7	13.88	8.60	3.24

$$F = \frac{\sum_{i=1}^{k} n_i (x_i - \bar{x})^2 / (k-1)}{\sum_{i=1}^{k} (n_i - 1)s_i^2 / (N-k)}$$

Here $N = \sum_{i=1}^{k} n_i$ denotes the combined sample size. If the population variances are equal F follows under the hypothesis of equal means an F-distribution with k-1 degrees of freedom for the numerator and N-k for the denominator. If the sample sizes are equal and the population variances (or the standard deviations) are unequal the actual size will exceed its nominal value, as can be seen in the last four lines of table 1. This effect is even stronger if the sample sizes are unequal and the smaller samples coincide with the bigger variances. But if the smaller sample sizes correspond with the smaller variances the reverse of this can be seen: the test becomes conservative, meaning that the actual probability of rejecting the hypothesis is lower than the nominal size α. This can be understood by looking at the denominator of the expression for F.

This F-test is based on the ratio of variances and therefore it seems natural to call it analysis of variance. But in this dissertation other tests will be considered that are based on quite different principles. Therefore from now on such tests will be looked upon as special cases of analysis of means, and the term analysis of variance will be avoided in this context.

The tests in chapter 2 originate from James (1951), Welch (1951) and Brown & Forsythe (1974). The test statistic used by James is very simple, but for the critical value a somewhat forbidding expression exists. Brown and Forsythe compared these tests by a simulation study. They used a first order Taylor expansion for the critical value of the method of James. Their conclusion was that this test was inferior when compared to their own and the method of Welch. In this dissertation a second order Taylor expansion will be considered. It will be demonstrated that in this case the test of James is superior to the other two in the sense of size control. None of the methods under consideration is uniformly more powerful than the other two, and therefore the method of James will be recommended with the second order Taylor approximation for the critical value. A practical disadvantage of this test is that its statistic does not result in the tail-probability with the help of a table or a standard statistical routine. But that problem can be overcome by a minor modification.

1.2. The Kruskal & Wallis test

When the results of the study on tests for the equality of several mean values (when the population variances are unequal) were presented at a conference, someone from the audience remarked: Why do you use such a complicated method? If I feel that the conditions for a classical test are not fulfilled I simply use the Kruskal & Wallis test.

Chapter 3 is a study on the behaviour of the Kruskal & Wallis test for normal populations with variance heterogeneity. The exact distribution of the test statistic is considered, as well as the popular χ^2 approximation and the more conservative Beta approximation by Wallace (1959). The results are compared with those for a nonparametric test that is specially designed for unequal variances.

The Kruskal & Wallis test is developed for the hypothesis that all samples come from the same continous distribution against the alternative that the location parameters are unequal. But unfortunately this test appears to be also sensitive for differences in the scale parameters. The test statistic is:

$$K = \frac{12}{N(N+1)} \sum_{i=1}^{k} n_i (\bar{R}_i - \bar{R})^2$$

R_{ij} denotes the rank of observation x_{ij} in the combined sample. $\bar{R}_i$ is the mean of the ranks in sample number i and $\bar{R} = \frac{N+1}{2}$. The formula for K suggests a transformation of the classical test that is to be applied to the ranks. So it will not be amazing to see in chapter 3 that the sensitivity of this test to unequal variances is similar to the sensitivity of the classical test. Therefore the Kruskal & Wallis test cannot be recommended in this situation if one uses it with the exact distribution of the test statistic, or if one uses the χ^2 approximation. The Beta approximation is somewhat conservative. Therefore it can handle a limited amount of variance heterogeneity, but the maximum ratio of the standard deviations should not exceed 3. For greater differences it is possible that the actual probability of declaring the means to be different when in fact they are equal will exceed the nominal level α. Another disadvantage is that if one uses this approximation the loss of power relative to the method of James can be quite impressive, especially if extreme means coincide with small variances.

1.3. An adaptive nonparametric test

During a conference on Robustness in Statistics, Tukey (1979) once remarked that a modern statistician who can use a computer should have a bouquet of tests for each of the most popular hypotheses. Some characteristics of the samples involved could then be used to determine which test would have optimal power in some particular situation. Such strategies usually involve adjustment of the level, but this is not necessary if the selection scheme uses information that is independent of the information used for the computation of the test statistic.

The Kruskal & Wallis test is a member of a large family of non-parametric methods that are designed for the hypothesis that k samples come from the same distribution. These tests can be used for the hypothesis that some location parameters are equal if the distributions involved are at least similar in shape and scale. If one uses the Kruskal & Wallis method for this purpose it is well known that the power will be optimal if the underlying distribution is logistic. More power can be obtained for distributions with shorter tails by using the Van der Waerden test, and for heavier tails the Mood & Brown test is a better choice [Hajek and Sidak (1967)].

In chapter 4 two adaptive tests will be discussed that are based on the selection scheme that is given in table 2.

Table 2: Selection scheme	
tail	method
light	Van der Waerden
medium	Kruskal & Wallis
heavy	Mood & Brown

One of these tests is a pure adaptive nonparametric method that uses independent information for the selection and the computation of the statistic. The other test involves some kind of moderate cheating concerning this independency in order to get some more power. It will be demonstrated that both methods have more power than any of the separate tests mentioned in table 2 if the underlying distribution is a mixture with equal occurencies of the following distributions: (1) uniform, (2) normal, (3) logistic, (4) double exponential and (5) Cauchy.

If this mixture would represent the situation that nothing about the distribution is known except the fact that it is symmetric, then these adaptive tests would be highly recommendable. But unfortunately the superiority of the power vanishes for small samples if one drops distributions (1) and (5). In that case the Kruskal & Wallis test is better for samples containing not more than 15 observations each.

The adaptive tests are not recommended in their present form. The moderate gain in power (for the above mentioned mixture of 5 distributions) is not worth the extra programming effort for the selection scheme. But two possible improvements are mentioned in chapter 4 that are still under consideration while this was written. So there is some hope that a better adaptive test will be found.

1.4. Some extreme outliers

In chapter 5 an error distribution will be considered that is $N(0,\sigma^2)$ with probability $1-\epsilon$ and $N(0,\theta\sigma^2)$ with probability ϵ. Since this distribution is intended to describe outliers the value of ϵ will be small and that of θ very large. This is a model for symmetric contamination; one-sided contamination will also be considered.

The behaviour of the classical method for one-way analysis of means will be compared with the behaviour of some alternatives that seem more promising with respect to their robustness against variance heterogeneity. The classical method cannot be recommended; one single outlier can remove all power from this test. The alternatives are the following: (1) Trimming, (2) Winsorizing, (3) Van der Waerden and (4) A method proposed by Huber (1981). Number (2) can handle a limited fraction of outliers, but it does not matter much how big they are. The other three are more robust and concerning the control over the chosen size their differences are very small. So the recommendation has to be based on the power and it will be demonstrated that Huber's method is the best choice.

Some attention will be given to two approaches that entered the study but that were discarded before the final simulation. One is based on a very robust method for regression problems that is called Least Median of Squares and that is proposed by Rousseeuw (1984). This method is suitable for testing in linear models as long as the predictors are continuous. But if the only predictor is nominal, so that the method reduces to regression with dummy-variables, the control over the chosen size becomes very unsatisfactory. The other method that was discarded was one based on adaptive nonparametric testing with optimal scores for the model-distribution. This involves simultaneous estimation of σ^2, θ and ϵ (for symmetric contamination) and it seems that the sample sizes needed for such an approach by far exceed the values that one usually meets in practice.

Table 3: Preliminary data description					
sample	minimum	Q_1	Q_2	Q_3	maximum
1	1.56	1.63	1.70	1.78	1.90
2	1.45	1.62	1.75	1.83	1.89
3	1.52	1.60	1.79	1.88	195

The simulations of chapters 2 and 5 will be combined, and this results in a somewhat disappointing conclusion: The test that is most robust against variance heterogeneity cannot even handle one single outlier, and Huber's method cannot be recommended if the variances are unequal. So the user has to perform some explorative data analysis before he can choose his test. But that is not very difficult here: look for instance at table 3 where Q_i denotes the quartiles so that Q_2 is the median. It is not difficult to recognise the outlier here: the analist probably just forgot to enter the decimal point once. Such tables can be considered as a preliminary data description for every analysis of means.

1.5. Simultaneous statistical inference

In chapter 6 a collection of hypotheses is considered: $\mu_i = \mu_j$ for i = 1 , ... , k and j = 1 , ... , i-1. The objective is to find tests for which the level α means the accepted probability of declaring any pair of means different when in fact they are equal. If the variances are equal, and in the absence of outliers, there are several approaches one can consider:

Fisher's (1935) Least Significant Difference test (modified by Hayter in 1986).

Pairwise comparisons based on the t-distribution with some level β that is a function of α and the number of pairs.

The Newman (1939), Duncan (1951) and Keuls (1952) Multiple Range tests with level α_p for a range containing p means. Suitable choices for α_p are proposed by Duncan (1955), Ryan (1960) and Welsch (1977).

Tukey's (1953) Wholly Significant Difference test that uses the studentized range distribution for pairwise comparisons.

The Multiple F-test that was proposed by Duncan (1951). Here the same values for α_p can be considered that were already mentioned for the Multiple Range test.

For all these methods alternatives will be considered that can handle variance heterogeneity or outliers. Tests with desirable properties are found for every approach that is based on pairwise comparisons, including the Least Significant Difference test. For unequal sample sizes the methods that are based on the Multiple Range test or the Multiple F-test have some very unpleasant properties, that do not disappear for equal sample sizes but unequal variances. However, these strategies can be succesfully adapted to error distributions with outliers as long as the design remains balanced.

2. Testing the equality of several means when the population variances are unequal

2.1. Introduction

We are interested in the situation where there are k independent sample means x_1 , ... , x_k from normally distributed populations. Denote the population means by μ_1 , ... , μ_k and the variances of their estimates by α_1 , ... , α_k. So we have $\alpha_i = \sigma_i^2/n_i$ where σ_i^2 is the variance within the i-th population and n_i is the i-th sample size. The null hypothesis to be tested is $H_0 : \mu_1 = ... = \mu_k$. For the moment we will suppose that the σ_i^2 are known. Unlike the situation in which the classical analysis of means test can be applied we will not suppose that $\sigma_i^2 = \sigma_j^2$ for i , j = 1 , ... , k. If we write $\omega_i = 1/\alpha_i$, $\omega = \sum_{i=1}^{k} \omega_i$, $\bar{x} = \sum_{i=1}^{k} \omega_i x_i / \omega$ and r = k - 1 it is well known that under H_0:

$$\sum_{i=1}^{k} \omega_i (x_i - \bar{x})^2 \simeq \chi_r^2$$

So it is no problem to test this null hypothesis. Now we will suppose that the population variances are unknown. If all the samples contain many observations it still is not a difficult problem. If we write $a_i = s_i^2/n_i$, $\nu_i = n_i - 1$, $w_i = 1/a_i$, $w = \sum_{i=1}^{k} w_i$ and $\bar{x} = \sum_{i=1}^{k} w_i x_i / w$ then $\sum_{i=1}^{k} w_i (x_i - \bar{x})^2$ will be approximately distributed as χ_r^2.

The topic of this chapter is the situation in which the population variances are unknown, and the samples are small.

2.2. The method of James

We will go back to the situation where the population variances are known. In that case we have:

$$Pr\left[\sum_{i=1}^{k}\omega_i(x_i-\bar{x})^2\leqslant\psi\right]=G_r(\psi)$$

Here $G_r(\psi)$ denotes the distribution function of a χ^2-distribution with r degrees of freedom. If the population variances are unknown, every α_i can be estimated by an a_i. Using these estimates James (1951) tried to find a function $h(a_i, ..., a_k, \psi)$ for which the following holds:

$$Pr\left[\sum_{i=1}^{k}w_i(x_i-\bar{x})^2\leqslant h(a_i, ..., a_k, \psi)\right]=G_r(\psi)$$

The function h will be implicitly defined if we write:

$$\int Pr\left[\sum_{i=1}^{k}w_i(x_i-\bar{x})^2\leqslant h(\vec{a},\psi)|\vec{a}\right]*Pr[d\vec{a}]=G_r(\psi)$$

Here the integration is from 0 to ∞ for every a_i. The first Pr-expression denotes the probability of the relation indicated for fixed a_i and $Pr[d\vec{a}]$ denotes the product of the probability differentials given by:

$$\frac{1}{\Gamma(\frac{1}{2}\nu_i)}\left(\frac{\nu_i a_i}{2\alpha_i}\right)^{\frac{1}{2}\nu_i-1}\exp\left(-\frac{\nu_i a_i}{2\alpha_i}\right)d\left(\frac{\nu_i a_i}{2\alpha_i}\right)$$

Using a Taylor expansion James found an approximation of order -2 in the ν_i. To give this expression we define the following two quantities:

$$R_{st}=\sum_{i=1}^{k}-\frac{1}{\nu_i^s}\left(\frac{w_i}{w}\right)^t$$

$$\chi_{2s}=[\chi^2(\alpha)]^s/(k-1)(k+1)...(k+2s-3)$$

Here $\chi^2(\alpha)$ denotes the percentage point of a χ^2-distributed variate with r degrees of freedom, having a tail probability of α. For the following it is important to realize that χ_{2s} depends on the chosen size α, whereas R_{st} is independent of α. After a good deal of algebra James found:

$$h_2(\alpha) = \chi^2 + \tfrac{1}{2}(3\chi_4 + \chi_2) + \sum_{i=1}^{k} \frac{1}{\nu_i}(1 - \frac{w_i}{w})^2$$

$$+ (\frac{1}{16}(3\chi_4 + \chi_2)^2(1 - \frac{k-3}{\chi^2})(\sum_{i=1}^{k} \frac{1}{\nu_i}(1 - \frac{w_i}{w})^2)^2$$

$$+ \tfrac{1}{2}(3\chi_4 + \chi_2)[(8R_{23} - 10R_{22} + 4R_{21} - 6R_{12}^2 + 8R_{12}R_{11} - 4R_{11}^2)$$

$$+ (2R_{23} - 4R_{22} + 2R_{21} - 2R_{12}^2 + 4R_{12}R_{11} - 2R_{11}^2)(\chi_2 - 1)$$

$$+ \tfrac{1}{4}(-R_{12}^2 + 4R_{12}R_{11} - 2R_{12}R_{10} - 4R_{11}^2 + 4R_{11}R_{10} - R_{10}^2)(3\chi_4 - 2\chi_2 - 1)]$$

$$+ (R_{23} - 3R_{22} + 3R_{21} - R_{20})(5\chi_6 + 2\chi_4 + \chi_2)$$

$$+ 3(R_{12}^2 - 4R_{23} + 6R_{22} - 4R_{21} + R_{20})(35\chi_8 + 15\chi_6 + 9\chi_4 + 5\chi_2)/16$$

$$+ (-2R_{22} + 4R_{21} - R_{20} + 2R_{12}R_{10} - 4R_{11}R_{10} + R_{10}^2)(9\chi_8 - 3\chi_6 - 5\chi_4 - \chi_2)/16$$

$$+ \tfrac{1}{4}(-R_{22} + R_{11}^2)(27\chi_8 + 3\chi_6 + \chi_4 + \chi_2)$$

$$+ \tfrac{1}{4}(R_{23} - R_{12}R_{11})(45\chi_8 + 9\chi_6 + 7\chi_4 + 3\chi_2))$$

The decision rule is to reject H_0 if $\sum_{i=1}^{k} w_i(x_i - \bar{x})^2 > h_2(\alpha)$. For $k = 2$ this test is identical to Welch's approximate solution of the Behrens-Fisher (1929) problem. This problem concerns the topic of this chapter, but it is limited to the case of two samples. Welch uses the test statistic:

$$V = \frac{x_1 - x_2}{\sqrt{s_1^2/n_1 + s_2^2/n_2}}$$

This test statistic is to be compared with a Student t-variable with f degrees of freedom, where f is computed as:

$$f = \frac{(s_1^2/n_1 + s_2^2/n_2)^2}{(s_1^2/n_1)^2/\nu_1 + (s_2^2/n_2)^2/\nu_2}$$

It may seem amazing that this simple test is equivalent to the very complicated second order James test in the case of two samples. But certain non-linear relations between the quantities R_{st} exist in the special case $k = 2$, so that the expression for $h_2(\alpha)$ reduces to the square of Welch's critical value.

For $k > 2$ James proposes to use the χ^2 test for large samples given in the introduction, and a very simple first order method for smaller samples. This method uses the critical value:

$$h_1(\alpha) = \chi^2 [1 + \frac{3\chi^2 + k + 1}{2(k^2 - 1)} \sum_{i=1}^{k} \frac{1}{\nu_i} (1 - \frac{w_i}{w})]$$

In his opinion it would involve too much numerical calculation to include the second correction term. But then it should be noted that in 1951 the computers were not the same as they are now.

2.3. The method of Welch

Welch (1951) started by using the same test statistic as James. For $k = 2$ this is the square of the statistic that Welch used for the Behrens-Fisher problem:

$$V^2 = \frac{(x_1 - x_2)^2}{s_1^2 / n_1 + s_2^2 / n_2} = \frac{w_1 w_2 (x_1 - x_2)^2}{w_1 + w_2} = \sum_{i=1}^{2} w_i (x_i - \bar{x})^2$$

Since Welch used a t-distribution for the two-sample test it was natural for him to try an F-distribution for the more general case of k samples. He started with the moment-generating function of $V^2 = \sum_{i=1}^{k} w_i (x_i - \bar{x})^2$ where $\bar{x} = \sum_{i=1}^{k} w_i x_i / w$. The moments of this statistic become infinite after a certain order, but Welch proceeded formally, as if the moment-generating function existed:

$$M(u) = E \exp[u \sum_{i=1}^{k} w_i (x_i - \bar{x})^2]$$

Here E denotes averaging over the joint distributions of x_i and s_i^2. Using a Taylor expansion, just like James did, Welch found:

$$M(u) = (1 - 2u)^{-\frac{1}{2}(k-1)} [1 + (2u(1 - 2u)^{-1} +$$

$$3u^2(1-2u)^{-2})(\sum_{i=1}^{k}\frac{1}{\nu_i}(1-\frac{\omega_i}{\sum_{i=1}^{k}\omega_i})^2)]$$

Therefore the cumulant-generating function of V^2 can be approximated by taking the natural logarithm of this expression:

$$K(u) = -\tfrac{1}{2}(k-1)\log_e(1-2u)+$$

$$[2u(1-2u)^{-1}+3u^2(1-2u)^{-2}][\sum_{i=1}^{k}\frac{1}{\nu_i}(1-\frac{\omega_i}{\sum_{i=1}^{k}\omega_i})^2]$$

Welch did not compare this result with the cumulant-generating function of an F-distributed variate, but he used a transformation:

$$G = [(k-1)+A/\nu_2]F$$

Here F has an F-distribution with f_1 and f_2 degrees of freedom. For f_1 Welch choose the natural value k - 1 and for G he found to order -1 in f_2 the cumulant-generating function:

$$K_G(u) = -\tfrac{1}{2}(k-1)\log_e(1-2u)+$$

$$\frac{1}{\nu_2}(A+2(k-1))u(1-2u)^{-1}+\frac{k^2-1}{f_2}u^2(1-2u)^{-2}$$

This is the same cumulant-generating function as that of the test statistic if the following two conditions hold:

$$\frac{1}{f_2}=\frac{3}{k^2-1}\sum_{i=1}^{k}\frac{1}{\nu_i}(1-\frac{\omega_i}{\sum_{i=1}^{k}\omega_i})^2$$

$$\frac{A}{f_2}=\frac{2(k-2)}{k+1}\sum_{i=1}^{k}\frac{1}{\nu_i}(1-\frac{\omega_i}{\sum_{i=1}^{k}\omega_i})^2$$

Therefore the test statistic $V^2=\sum_{i=1}^{k}w_i(x_i-\bar{x})^2$ is approximately distributed as $[(k-1)+A/f_2]F$ where the parameters f_1 and f_2 of the F-distribution are given as follows: $f_1 = k - 1$ and f_2 is with A implicitly defined in the above given two equations. In order to get a statistic that is approximately distributed as an F-distribution Welch modified the simple form of V^2 into:

$$W = \frac{\sum_{i=1}^{k} w_i (x_i - \bar{x})^2 / (k-1)}{1 + \frac{2(k-2)}{k^2-1} \sum_{i=1}^{k} \frac{1}{\nu_i} (1 - \frac{w_i}{\sum_{i=1}^{k} w_i})^2}$$

This statistic can be approximated by an F-distribution with $f_1 = k - 1$ and f_2 degrees of freedom, where f_2 is given by:

$$f_2 = [\frac{3}{k^2-1} \sum_{i=1}^{k} \frac{1}{\nu_i} (1 - \frac{w_i}{\sum_{i=1}^{k} w_i})^2]^{-1}$$

Since f_2 will usually not be an integer it should be rounded to the nearest one before a table for the F-distribution can be used for this test. It can be shown that this method is equivalent to the method of James to order -1 in the ν_i.

2.4. The method of Brown and Forsythe

If we may assume that the population variances are equal, H_0 can be tested by classical one-way analysis of means, using the statistic:

$$F = \frac{\sum_{i=1}^{k} n_i (x_i - \bar{x})^2 / (k-1)}{\sum_{i=1}^{k} (n_i-1) s_i^2 / (N-k)}$$

Here $N = \sum_{i=1}^{k} n_i$ and $\bar{x} = \sum_{i=1}^{k} n_i x_i / N$. Brown and Forsythe replaced the denominator of this formula by an expression that has the same expectation as the numerator when H_0 holds. Their test statistic becomes:

$$F^* = \frac{\sum_{i=1}^{k} n_i (x_i - \bar{x})^2}{\sum_{i=1}^{k} (1 - n_i / N) s_i^2}$$

This statistic is approximated by an F-distribution with f_1 and f_2 degrees of freedom, where $f_1 = k - 1$. For finding f_2 Brown and Forsythe used the Satterthwaite (1941) technique. Their result is:

$$f_2 = [\sum_{i=1}^{k} c_i^2 / \nu_i]^{-1} \text{ where}$$

$$c_i = (1 - n_i / N) s_i^2 / [\sum_{i=1}^{k} (1 - n_i / N) s_i^2]$$

If $k = 2$ the W and F^* test give (just like the James method) results that are equivalent to Welch's approximate solution of the Behrens-Fisher problem. Although Scheffé (1944) has already proven that exact solutions of this type cannot be found, a simulation study of Wang (1971) has shown that the approximate solution for $k = 2$ gives excellent control over the size of the test, whatever the value of the nuisance parameter $\theta = \sigma_1^2 / \sigma_2^2$ may be.

2.5. Results of previous simulation studies

Brown and Forsythe compared their test with the classical analysis of means test, the first order method of James and the test of Welch. Their conclusions were as follows:

-    If the population variances are unequal then the difference between the nominal size and the actual probability of an error of the first kind can be considerable for the classical analysis of means and the first order method of James, even when the differences between the population variances are relatively small.

-    The power of the tests of Welch and Brown & Forsythe is only slightly smaller than the power of the classical analysis of means test when the population variances are equal.

- If extreme means correspond to small variances then the method of Welch is more powerful than the test of Brown & Forsythe. And if extreme means correspond to the bigger variances then the method of Brown & Forsythe has more power, as can be seen by comparing the numerators of the test statistics:

Welch: $\sum_{i=1}^{k} w_i (x_i - \bar{x})^2/(k-1)$, where $w_i = n_i/s_i^2$, $\bar{x} = \sum_{i=1}^{k} w_i x_i/w$

and $w = \sum_{i=1}^{k} w_i$.

Brown & Forsythe: $\sum_{i=1}^{k} n_i (x_i - \bar{x})^2$, where $\bar{x} = \sum_{i=1}^{k} n_i x_i/N$ and

$N = \sum_{i=1}^{k} n_i$

Ekbohm (1976) published a similar simulation study. He also left out the second order method of James, but included a test of Scheffe' (1959). His conclusions agree with the results of Brown and Forsythe. Ekbohm found, however, something extra. He recognized the possibility that an important difference between two means might not be found because of a big variance in a third population. Dealing adequately with this problem is a topic of simultaneous statistical inference. Serious attention to this problem will be given in the last chapter.

2.6. An example

Data from three groups, where the assumption of variance homogeneity seemed unreasonable, were submitted to the methods given in the previous sections. After a suitabe scaling the data were:

Sample 1: 1.72 -1.56 0.98 0.31 0.92

Sample 2: 2.51 2.56 2.17 1.69 1.83 1.04 1.34 3.38 2.98 1.79 1.88 2.05

Sample 3: 2.50 7.33 -5.34 -18.64 0.04 4.27 4.78 -5.52 -3.11 -8.84 -0.13 -0.19 15.55 13.36 2.97

These data can be summarized as follows:

$$x_1 = 0.469 \quad s_1 = 1.242 \quad n_1 = 5$$
$$x_2 = 2.102 \quad s_2 = 0.665 \quad n_2 = 12$$
$$x_3 = 0.601 \quad s_3 = 8.532 \quad n_3 = 15$$

The hypothesis of interest concers the equality of the population means. Normality seems a reasonable assumption, but variance homogeneity can not be assumed. Welch's test resulted in $W = 3.757$ with 2 and 10 degrees of freedom. The critical value of the F-statistic with these parameters and $\alpha = 0.05$ is given as 4.10. So the hypothesis can not be rejected at this level, but the difference between the test statistic and the critical value is small. For the James second order test one has to compute not only the statistic, but also the critical value. In order to get a more interpretable result, the tail-probability of the test was computed. This yielded a value of 0.066 wich just exceeds the size of the test. So the results of the tests by Welch and James are similar. Since these tests originate from the same statistic, this is just what one might expect.

The test by Brown and Forsythe gives $F^* = 0.439$ with 2 and 15 degrees of freedom. Here the critical value of the F-statistic $= 3.68$ so the hypothesis can not be rejected. The acceptance of the hypothesis is far more convincing than with the other two methods. This is in accordance with the fact that the extreme mean of the second sample coincides with the smallest standard deviation.

Since the variance in the third group is much bigger than the other two variances it is interesting to examine what will happen if the third group is removed and the hypothesis of equal population means is restricted to the first two samples. Here Welch's method yields $W = 7.663$ with 1 and 5 degrees of freedom. The critical value of the F-statistic is 6.61 so the hypothesis is rejected. The method of James gives a tail probability of 0.038, resulting in the same conclusion. The test of Brown and Forsythe gives exactly the same results as the method of Welch, which is just what one might expect since they are identical for two samples. Because we have only two samples this is an example of the Behrens-Fisher problem and the hypothesis of equal population means can also be tested with Welch's approximate t-solution. Here the statistic V = -2.768 with 5 degrees of freedom. This is essentially the same result as that of the Brown & Forsythe test or Welch's solution for the k-sample problem. We have $V^2 = F' = W$ and the parameter of the t-distributed statistic is equal to the number of degrees of freedom for the denominator in the F-distributed statistics.

In this example the significant difference between the first two population means is hidden because of the big standard deviation in the third group. Such problems are well known in the classical case of equal population variances but unequal sample sizes. Allowing the variances to be unequal can make things worse in this respect. The researcher should consider carefully before deciding to perform an overall test in this situation. In many cases a couple of pairwise comparisons might be a better choice.

2.7. The difference between the nominal size and the actual probability of rejecting a true null hypothesis

For this study pseudo-random numbers were generated from k normal distributions. Since we are interested in the behaviour of the tests under the null hypothesis all population means were equal and without any loss of generality their value was set to zero. The samples were generated using the Box and Muller (1958) technique [see appendix 1]. For the tests of Brown & Forsythe and Welch the probability function of the F-distribution was computed following suggestions of Johnson & Kotz (1970) [see appendix 2]. For computing $h_1(\alpha)$ and $h_2(\alpha)$ in respectively the first and second order test of James one needs the inverse χ^2-distribution. The method for computing this function can be found in Stegun & Abramowitz (1964) [see appendix 3]. For k the values 4 and 6 were chosen. The nominal size p is given three values: 0.10, 0.05 and 0.01. The results of this simulation study are given in tables 1, 2 and 3. The actual relative frequency of rejecting a true null hypothesis has of course not necessarily the same value, but one might expect it not to differ too greatly from p. An acceptable difference seems to be 2σ, where σ is the standard deviation of a

Table 1: Actual size with nominal size = 10%					
sample size	sigma	Br-Fo	James1	James2	Welch
4,4,4,4	1,1,1,1	7.72	12.96	10.28	9.96
	1,2,2,3	9.84	13.88	11.08	11.36
4,6,8,10	1,1,1,1	8.08	11.44	9.96	10.28
	1,2,2,3	9.56	10.00	9.12	9.16
	3,2,2,1	10.24	12.64	10.24	10.92
10,10,10,10	1,1,1,1	9.60	10.68	10.44	10.48
	1,2,2,3	10.80	10.40	9.72	9.92
10,15,15,20	1,1,1,1	9.04	9.64	9.52	9.52
	1,2,2,3	10.68	10.40	10.16	10.24
	3,2,2,1	10.12	10.24	9.72	9.84
20,20,20,20	1,1,1,1	9.20	9.32	9.28	9.28
	1,2,2,3	10.80	10.04	9.96	9.96
4,4,4,4,4,4	1,1,1,1,1,1	8.04	15.04	9.84	11.52
	1,1,2,2,3,3	9.44	16.56	11.12	13.08
4,6,8,10,12,14	1,1,1,1,1,1	8.56	11.52	9.56	10.20
	1,1,2,2,3,3	10.16	10.76	8.88	9.48
	3,3,2,2,1,1	10.32	12.20	9.84	11.12
10,10,10,10,10,10	1,1,1,1,1,1	10.48	11.60	11.00	11.20
	1,1,2,2,3,3	12.48	12.12	11.00	11.76
10,10,15,15,20,20	3,3,2,2,1,1	11.44	10.16	9.40	9.92

binomial distribution. In this case we have $\sigma = \sqrt{pq/n}$, where q = 1 - p. The number of simulations n for each case was 2500. So we have σ_{10} = 0.600%, σ_5 = 0.436% and σ_1 = 0.199%. Let d be the estimated size of the test minus the nominal size and this difference divided by the appropriate value of σ. Then we may call the behaviour of the test conservative if d < -2, accurate if -2 $\leqslant$ d < 2 and progressive if 2 $\leqslant$ d. Table 4 gives the occurances of various categories for d. The regions for conservative, accurate and progressive behaviour are separated by double lines. From table 4 we learn that the first order method of James has an extremely progressive behaviour and should therefore not

Table 2: Actual size with nominal size = 5%					
sample size	sigma	Br-Fo	James1	james2	Welch
4,4,4,4	1,1,1,1	3.48	7.40	4.64	4.52
	1,2,2,3	4.80	8.56	5.48	5.84
4,6,8,10	1,1,1,1	4.16	6.44	4.56	4.96
	1,2,2,3	5.16	5.56	4.72	4.72
	3,2,2,1	5.64	7.48	5.64	6.32
10,10,10,10	1,1,1,1	4.64	5.60	5.36	5.36
	1,2,2,3	6.12	5.92	5.52	5.56
10,15,15,20	1,1,1,1	4.68	5.04	4.88	4.88
	1,2,2,3	5.96	5.12	5.00	5.00
	3,2,2,1	4.84	5.00	4.72	4.84
20,20,20,20	1,1,1,1	4.80	4.88	4.80	4.84
	1,2,2,3	5.96	4.60	4.48	4.48
4,4,4,4,4,4	1,1,1,1,1,1	3.32	8.92	5.28	6.12
	1,1,2,2,3,3	4.64	10.40	6.12	6.88
4,6,8,10,12,14	1,1,1,1,1,1	4.32	6.80	5.04	6.04
	1,1,2,2,3,3	5.88	5.36	3.92	4.72
	3,3,2,2,1,1	5.72	7.80	5.40	6.72
10,10,10,10,10,10	1,1,1,1,1,1	5.12	6.60	5.84	6.00
	1,1,2,2,3,3	6.84	6.72	5.76	6.24
10,10,15,15,20,20	1,1,2,2,3,3	7.24	5.20	4.76	5.00
	3,3,2,2,1,1	6.60	5.60	4.88	5.24

be used. Welch's test has about the same tendency to progressiveness as the method of Brown & Forsythe, but of these tests only Brown & Forsythe can also demonstrate a conservative behaviour if the pattern of sample sizes and variances makes this possible. The second order method of James is clearly the best in this respect. The only entry in this table that suggests a really progressive behaviour originates from table 3, where we can see that the actual size is estimated as 1.96% while the nominal size = 1%. This occured with six very small samples, containing only 4 observations each. Besides this a very slight

Table 3: Actual size with nominal size = 1%					
sample size	sigma	Br-Fo	James1	James2	Welch
4,4,4,4	1,1,1,1	0.44	2.32	0.84	0.76
	1,2,2,3	0.96	3.12	1.32	1.12
4,6,8,10	1,1,1,1	0.64	1.80	1.20	1.28
	1,2,2,3	1.00	1.60	1.00	1.00
	3,2,2,1	1.24	3.08	1.52	1.68
10,10,10,10	1,1,1,1	1.24	1.24	0.88	0.92
	1,2,2,3	1.72	1.28	0.84	0.92
10,15,15,20	1,1,1,1	0.92	1.28	1.12	1.16
	1,2,2,3	1.48	1.36	1.28	1.32
	3,2,2,1	1.44	1.16	0.96	1.00
20,20,20,20	1,1,1,1	1.12	1.00	0.92	0.92
	1,2,2,3	1.48	0.84	0.76	0.76
4,4,4,4,4,4	1,1,1,1,1,1	0.44	3.44	1.12	1.44
	1,1,2,2,3,3	1.04	4.36	1.96	2.36
4,6,8,10,12,14	1,1,1,1,1,1	0.60	2.00	1.28	1.44
	1,1,2,2,3,3	1.48	1.28	0.68	0.88
	3,3,2,2,1,1	1.48	2.76	1.44	2.16
10,10,10,10,10,10	1,1,1,1,1,1	0.84	1.72	1.24	1.36
	1,1,2,2,3,3	2.12	1.56	1.16	1.32
10,10,15,15,20,20	1,1,2,2,3,3	1.92	0.88	0.76	0.84
	3,3,2,2,1,1	1.68	1.24	1.08	1.20

suggestion of progressiveness occured three times for the second order method of James and these occurences have in common that a relatively big standard deviation was combined with a very small sample size of 4 observations. So the conclusion of this section can be that as far as the control over the chosen size is concerned, the second order method of James is the best.

Table 4: Summary of tables 1, 2 and 3				
	Br–Fo	James1	James2	Welch
$d < -3$	5			
$-3 \leqslant d < -2$	3		1	
$-2 \leqslant d < -1$	6	1	8	6
$-1 \leqslant d < 1$	23	19	36	31
$1 \leqslant d < 2$	7	11	14	10
$2 \leqslant d < 3$	10	6	3	9
$3 \leqslant d < 4$	3	6		3
$4 \leqslant d < 5$	4	5	1	1
$5 \leqslant d$	2	15		3

2.8. The power of the tests

Table 5 is similar to the tables in the previous section, though of course here the equality of the population means is dropped. The number of replications for each entry is 2500. Table 5 suggests the following concusions:

- None of the methods is uniformly more powerful than the other two.

- If extreme means coincide with big variances the power of the test of Brown & Forsythe is superior, as was already found by the originators of this method. It can also be seen that the tests of James and Welch are more powerful if extreme means coincide with small variances.

In Dijkstra and Werter (1981) more tables like this can be found, where the first order method of James is left out. These tables suggest the same conclusions concerning the power and the control over the chosen size. Table 6 is a summary of table 5. For each test the mean percentage of rejections was computed in three categories: EMSV (Extreme Means with Small Variances), EMBV (Extreme Means with Big Variances) and EQV (EQual Variances). From table 6 we can get the impression that Welch's test is slightly more powerful than the

SS	mean	sigma	Br-Fo	James1	James2	Welch
Table 5: Estimated power with nominal size = 5%						
A	3,0,0,0	1,1,1,1	93.80	91.92	86.84	86.48
	$5,0,0,\frac{1}{2}$		100	99.96	99.94	99.68
	3,0,0,0	1,2,2,3	31.16	72.04	60.28	59.88
	0,0,0,3		30.64	28.72	22.72	22.68
	$5,0,0,\frac{1}{2}$		75.24	98.60	97.08	97.08
	$\frac{1}{2},0,0,5$		63.52	52.44	43.72	43.44
B	3,0,0,0	1,1,1,1	98.80	95.40	92.88	93.52
	3,0,0,0	1,2,2,3	54.28	89.12	86.96	87.28
	0,0,0,3		73.76	55.24	50.40	51.32
	$5,0,0,\frac{1}{2}$		97.88	99.96	99.88	99.88
	$\frac{1}{2},0,0,5$		98.92	92.92	91.48	91.56
	3,0,0,0	3,2,2,1	34.80	30.00	24.12	25.76
	0,0,0,3		67.04	97.04	94.64	95.40
	$5,0,0,\frac{1}{2}$		71.20	60.60	51.64	54.28
	$\frac{1}{2},0,0,5$		95.88	100	100	100
C	3,0,0,0,0,0	1,1,1,1,1,1	99.16	94.72	91.60	93.76
		1,1,2,2,3,3	48.96	93.72	90.76	92.44
		3,3,2,2,1,1	33.56	29.92	23.96	27.12

SS	sample size
A	4,4,4,4
B	4,6,8,10
C	4,6,8,10,12,14

second order method of James, and that the first order method of James has considerably more power that the second order method. But these results are misleading, because Welch's test has a slight tendency to progressiveness and the first order method of James has an extremely progressive behaviour (see table 4). The test of Brown & Forsythe seems a bit more powerful that the other three if the

Table 6: Summary of table 5				
category	Br–Fo	James1	James2	Welch
EMSV	67.21	92.93	89.94	90.24
EMBV	58.06	49.98	43.97	45.17
EQV	97.94	95.50	92.74	93.36

variances are equal. This is not amazing, because the numerator in the test statistic of Brown & Forsythe is the same as that of the classical one-way analysis of means test. And the latter is the best choice in the case of normal populations and variance homogeneity.

2.9. A modification of the second order test of James

Since the second order method of James gives the best control over the actual size, and none of the tests is uniformly the most powerful, this method is recommended for implementation is statistical software packages. However there seem to be two disadvantages, namely the very complicated algorithm and the fact that the result of applying this test can only be "H_0 accepted" or "H_0 rejected". Using the methods of Welch or Brown & Forsythe the value of the test statistic gives, in combination with a table or a numerical procedure, the tail probability for the test. This is of course useful information and it would be nice if the method of James could be modified so that the result would be the appropriate tail probability. This can easily be achieved by solving the equation $f(\alpha) = 0$, where:

$$f(\alpha) = \sum_{i=1}^{k} w_i (x_i - \bar{x})^2 - h_2(\alpha)$$

with $w_i = n_i / s_i^2$, $\bar{x} = \sum_{i=1}^{k} w_i x_i / w$ and $w = \sum_{i=1}^{k} w_i$. Because h_2 is monotonous in α, an acceptable precision of 10^{-3} can be expected in less than ten function evaluations. Please note that many parts of the formula for $h_2(\alpha)$ are independent of α, and should therefore be evaluated only once. In the iterative process it is only necessary te recompute χ_{2s}

every time.

This modified second order test of James was tried on a Burroughs B7700 computer. The average amount of processing time needed for common cases was about 0.026 sec. We may conclude therefore that modern computers are fast enough to accept this rather complicated method, even in its iterative version. Since this test of James is superior to its competitors, it should be implemented in statistical packages such as BMDP, SAS and SPSS.

3. Using the Kruskal & Wallis test with normal distributions and unequal variances

3.1. Introduction

Consider k samples with sample size n_i for i = 1 , ... , k. The observations are x_{ij} for j = 1 , ... , n_i and let the rank of every observation be denoted as R_{ij}. In the case of equal observations the mean of their rank is used. The test statistic of Kruskal & Wallis (1952) is given as:

$$K = \frac{12}{N(N+1)} \sum_{i=1}^{k} n_i (\bar{R}_i - \bar{R})^2$$

Here $N = \sum_{i=1}^{k} n_i$ and $\bar{R} = \frac{N+1}{2}$. $\bar{R}_i$ denotes the mean of the ranks within the i-th group. With K we can test the hypothesis H_0 that all samples come from the same population. This test is frequently used for a non-parametric analysis of means, because it is sensitive to shifts in the location parameters. If the distribitions are symmetric the test statistic does not seem to be very much influenced by inequality of the shape parameters. Therefore one might be tempted to use the Kruskal & Wallis test for the hypothesis H_0^* that the population means are equal in the case of normal distributions with possibly unequal variances. The suggestion that this might work lies mainly in the fact that for symmetrical distributions the median and the mean of a sample have the same expectation. And the primary goal of the Kruskal & Wallis test is the detection of a shift in the medians.

3.2. The distribution of K under H_0

Under H_0 the test statistic K is asymptotically distributed as χ^2 with k -1 degrees of freedom. For moderate samples the approximation seems to be reasonable (Hajek and Sidak, 1967) and this test is commonly used if all the samples contain at least 5 observations. For very small samples the exact distribution of K is tabulated (Iman, Quade and Alexander, 1975). An alternative for χ^2 or these tables is given by Wallace (1959). He has shown that K is approximately distributed under H_0 as Beta(p,q), where the parameters p and q are given as p = $\frac{1}{2}$ (k - 1)d and q = $\frac{1}{2}$ (N - k)d. The constant d is given by:

$$d = 1 - \frac{6}{5} \frac{N+1}{N-1} \cdot \frac{1}{\frac{6}{5} + \frac{N}{1-T}}$$

$$T = \frac{N(N+1)}{2(k-1)(N-k)} \left(\sum_{i=1}^{k} \frac{1}{n_i} - \frac{k^2}{N} \right)$$

The behaviour of the Kruskal & Wallis test with the χ^2 and Beta approximation under the hypothesis H_0^* that all the population means are equal for normal populations with unequal variances will be examined further in this chapter. Some attention will be given to small samples in combination with tables for the exact distribution of the test statistic under H_0, while we are using it for H_0^*.

3.3. Other tests for the hypothesis H_0^*

For testing the equality of several means from normal populations one usually performs a classical one-way analysis of means. For this method the population variances have to be equal. Simulation studies of Brown & Forsythe (1974) and Ekbohm (1976) have already demonstrated that this test is not robust against variance heterogeneity. An exact test with a reasonable power, that is based on the F-distribution, does not exist for the hypothesis of equal means from normal populations under variance heterogeneity. Scheffé did already prove that for k = 2 no symmetrical t-test can be found. In this context symmetry means that the test is insensitive to permutations within the samples. And since the order in which the observations in a sample are submitted to the analysis has no meaning for the researcher, an asymmetrical test seems undesirable. Another disadvantage of asymmetrical tests is that they usually have little power if the sample sizes are very different. In the two-sample case with unequal population variances we have the Behrens-Fisher problem and for this Bartlett suggested the following asymmetrical test that he did not publish, but that was mentioned by Welch (1938). Let the sample sizes be n_1 and n_2 and suppose $n_1 \leqslant n_2$. Let:

$$d_i = x_{1i} - \sum_{j=1}^{n_2} c_{ij} x_{2j}$$

Then the variables d_i have a multivariate normal distribution. Scheffe' showed that necessary and sufficient conditions that they have the same mean δ and equal variances σ^2 are $\sum_{j=1}^{n_2} c_{ij} = 1$ and $\sum_{k=1}^{n_2} c_{ik} c_{jk} = c^2 \delta_{ij}$ for some constant c^2, where $\delta_{ii} = 1$ and $\delta_{ij} = 0$ if $i \neq j$. If these conditions are met we can construct the following t-test:

$$\frac{\sqrt{n_1}(L - \delta)}{\sqrt{Q/(n_1 - 1)}} \simeq t_{n_1 - 1}$$

Here $L = \sum_{i=1}^{n_1} d_i / n_1$ and $Q = \sum_{i=1}^{n_1} (d_i - L)^2$. In this situation $\sqrt{n_1}(L - \delta)/\sigma$ is standard normally distributed, and Q/σ^2 is distributed as χ^2 with $n_1 - 1$ degrees of freedom, and they are independent of each other.

Bartlett's solution consists of taking $c_{ij} = \delta_{ij}$, so that we have essentially a paired t-test for a random permutation within the samples, where $n_2 - n_1$ observations are completely ignored from the biggest sample. Scheffe' improved this test a little by minimizing the expected length l of the confidence interval for δ:

$$E(l) = \frac{2 t_{n_1 - 1}(\alpha) \sigma E \sqrt{Q/\sigma^2}}{\sqrt{n_1(n_1 - 1)}}$$

Here $t_\nu(\alpha)$ denotes the critical value for a t-distributed variate with ν degrees of freedom having a tail probability α for a two-sided test. Scheffe' found that the minimum was reached if:

$$c_{ij} = \delta_{ij} \sqrt{n_1/n_2} - \frac{1}{\sqrt{n_1 n_2}} + \frac{1}{n_2} \quad \text{if } j \leqslant n_1$$

$$c_{ij} = \frac{1}{n_2} \quad \text{if } j > n_1$$

Later (1970) Scheffe' stated that Welch's approximate t-solution for the Behrens–Fisher problem resulted in even shorter confidence intervals for δ than this optimal member of the above mentioned asymmetrical family produces. He mentioned his own result under the header: An impractical solution. In referring to his test he gave as his opinion:

> These articles were written before I had much consulting experience, and since then I have never recommended the solution in practice. The reason is that the estimate s_d requires putting in random order the elements of the larger sample, and the value of s_d and hence the length of the interval depends very much on the result of this randomization of the data. The effect of this in practice would be deplorable.

So we can not have a symmetrical F-test for H_o^* and it seems reasonable not to accept an asymmetrical test. Therefore the only alternative for a nonparametric test can be an approximation. In the previous chapter we saw that the second order method of James gave the user better control over the chosen size than some other tests, and none of these tests was uniformly most powerful. Therefore it seems interesting to compare the Kruskal & Wallis test with the test by James for normal populations with possibly unequal variances.

3.4. The nominal and estimated size

The second order method of James is already extensively described in the previous section. Tables 1, 2 and 3 give the estimated size for various patterns sample sizes and standard deviations. The Kruskal & Wallis test is considered with the Beta (that will be denoted as β in the tables) and the χ^2 approximation, and these results are compared with the results of the James test. For the nominal size the values 0.10, 0.05 and 0.01 were chosen. Since every entry of these tables is based on 2500 replications, the estimated sizes have the following standard deviations: $\sigma_{10} = 0.600\%$, $\sigma_5 = 0.436\%$ and $\sigma_1 = 0.199\%$. For the Beta approximation we need the Beta distribution function that is defined as follows:

Table 1: Actual size with nominal size = 10%				
sample size	sigma	KW β	KW χ^2	James2
4,4,4,4	1,1,1,1	5.88	9.24	10.28
	1,2,2,3	7.68	10.44	11.08
4,6,8,10	1,1,1,1	3.08	9.08	9.96
	1,2,2,3	2.60	6.52	9.12
	3,2,2,1	8.00	18.84	10.24
10,10,10,10	1,1,1,1	6.76	8.32	9.84
	1,2,2,3	5.00	11.04	9.72
4,4,4,4,4,4	1,1,1,1,1,1	6.76	8.32	9.84
	1,1,2,2,3,3	8.68	10.36	11.12
4,6,8,10,12,14	1,1,1,1,1,1	3.68	8.40	9.56
	1,1,2,2,3,3	2.04	5.12	8.88
	3,3,2,2,1,1	10.08	16.92	9.84
10,10,10,10,10,10	1,1,1,1,1,1	4.80	9.72	11.00
	1,1,2,2,3,3	6.64	11.88	11.00

$$Beta\,(p\,,q\,,x\,)= \frac{\Gamma(p+q+2)}{\Gamma(p+1)\Gamma(q+1)} \int\limits_0^x t^p\,(1-t\,)^q\,dt$$

This function is definied for $0 \leqslant x \leqslant 1$, $p > -1$ and $q > -1$. For the computation algorithm 179 from the Communications of the ACM was used, that was written by Ludwig (1962). The speed of this algorithm was improved following suggestions by Pike and Hill (1963).

Table 4 is a summary of the tables 1, 2 and 3 where the value of d is defined as the estimated size minus the nominal value and this result devided by the appropriate standard deviation. If $d < -2$ we may call the behaviour of the test conservative, if $-2 \leqslant d < 2$ the test seems accurate, and if $2 \leqslant d$ the test shows a progressive behaviour. These categories are separated in table 4 by double lines. At first sight the following conclusions may be drawn from this table:

- The Kruskal & Wallis test with the Beta approximation has a strong tendency towards conservatism. There are patterns for the

Table 2: Actual size with nominal size = 5%				
sample size	sigma	KW β	KW χ^2	James2
4,4,4,4	1,1,1,1	3.08	3.40	4.64
	1,2,2,3	4.40	4.76	5.84
4,6,8,10	1,1,1,1	1.52	3.80	4.56
	1,2,2,3	1.20	2.60	4.72
	3,2,2,1	4.68	7.96	5.64
10,10,10,10	1,1,1,1	1.64	4.28	5.36
	1,2,2,3	2.64	5.68	5.52
4,4,4,4,4,4	1,1,1,1,1,1	3.44	3.08	5.28
	1,1,2,2,3,3	4.92	4.60	6.12
4,6,8,10,12,14	1,1,1,1,1,1	1.64	3.28	5.04
	1,1,2,2,3,3	0.92	1.92	3.92
	3,3,2,2,1,1	5.96	9.36	5.40
10,10,10,10,10,10	1,1,1,1,1,1	2.08	4.80	5.84
	1,1,2,2,3,3	3.04	6.60	5.76

sample sizes and variances where the behaviour seems accurate, but this occured only 12 times against 30 occurences of a value of d going below -2.

- If we use the χ^2 approximation with the Kruskal & Wallis test the conservatism seems to lessen. There are more cases where the behaviour seems accurate, but a new problem arises: Patterns of sample sizes and variances exist for which the test seems progressive.

- The second order method of James behaves reasonably except once, where the variances are unequal and all six of the samples contain only 4 observations. This situation was already discussed in the previous chapter.

Since the results for the Kruskal & Wallis test with both approximations are not satisfactory in this study with unequal variances, it is sensible to have a closer look at the tables 1, 2 and 3. In table 5 a small section of these tables is given in order to demonstrate a

Table 3: Actual size with nominal size = 1%				
sample size	sigma	KW β	KW χ^2	James2
4,4,4,4	1,1,1,1	0.76	0.16	0.84
	1,2,2,3	1.08	0.24	1.32
4,6,8,10	1,1,1,1	0.28	0.28	1.20
	1,2,2,3	0.20	0.28	1.00
	3,2,2,1	0.88	1.04	1.52
10,10,10,10	1,1,1,1	0.36	0.76	0.88
	1,2,2,3	0.52	0.96	0.84
4,4,4,4,4,4	1,1,1,1,1,1	0.60	0.16	1.12
	1,1,2,2,3,3	1.24	0.36	1.96
4,6,8,10,12,14	1,1,1,1,1,1	0.36	0.48	1.28
	1,1,2,2,3,3	0.32	0.36	0.68
	3,3,2,2,1,1	1.56	2.28	1.44
10,10,10,10,10,10	1,1,1,1,1,1	0.40	0.68	1.24
	1,1,2,2,3,3	0.72	1.16	1.16

Table 4: Summary of tables 1, 2 and 3			
	KW β	KW χ^2	James2
$d \leqslant -3$	27	14	
$-3 \leqslant d < -2$	3	4	1
$-2 \leqslant d < -1$	4	5	4
$-1 \leqslant d < 1$	5	10	20
$1 \leqslant d < 2$	1	2	13
$2 \leqslant j < 3$	2		3
$3 \leqslant d < 4$		2	
$4 \leqslant d < 5$			1
$5 \leqslant d$		5	

remarkable effect. This section consists of all the results for sample sizes 4, 6, 8, 10, 12 and 14.

Table 5: Kruskal & Wallis, $n_i = 4,6,8,10,12,14$						
	β			χ^2		
sigma	10%	5%	1%	10%	5%	1%
1,1,1,1,1,1	3.68	1.64	0.36	8.40	3.28	0.48
1,1,2,2,3,3	2.04	0.92	0.32	5.12	1.92	0.36
3,3,2,2,1,1	10.08	5.96	1.56	16.92	9.36	2.28

What do we learn from table 5? If the variances are equal then both approximations yield a conservative test. We have here the situation where the Kruskal & Wallis test should behave properly (all samples come from the same population) so the only source of this deviation can be that the approximations are not very good for these sample sizes. Asymptotically the approximations are good, and if all the samples contain 10 observations at least the χ^2 approximation shows far better results in the tables 1, 2 and 3. But these samples, or at least some of them, are simply too small.

If we take this conservatism into account it is interesting to note that in the second line, where the bigger sample sizes coincide with the bigger variances, every entry is lower than the corresponding one in the first line. And in the third line we have the reverse of this: the bigger sample sizes coincide with the smaller variances, and all the entries are higher than the corresponding ones in the first line. More than that: The nominal size is exceeded everywhere in the last line. For the Beta approximation only a little, but for the χ^2 approximation considerably.

In the next section more attention to this effect will be given, but now we can reach a preliminary conclusion: The Kruskal & Wallis test is not recommended for normal populations with possibly unequal variances. If this test is used with a χ^2 approximation deviations from the nominal size can occur in both directions. If a β approximation is used, the test will be conservative if the variances are equal, and very conservative if the bigger sample sizes coincide with the bigger variances. If one is willing to accept conservatism one is usually confronted with unsatisfactory power. This is also the case here, as will be seen later in this chapter.

3.5. The effect of unequal sample sizes and variances

The effect of the sample size and variance on the control over the chosen size seems to be independent of the chosen approximation. If a correction for the conservatism with small samples due to the approximation is made, we saw in the previous section that the behaviour of the test is consistently conservative if the bigger sample sizes coincide with the bigger variances and progressive if it is the other way around. For very small samples the critical levels for the test statistic K are tabulated by Iman, Quade and Alexander (1975). These results are exact; no approximation is involved. In table 6 the effect of unequal sample sizes and variances is demonstrated for the exact Kruskal & Wallis test.

Table 6: Kruskal & Wallis (exact)				
sample size	sigma	10%	5%	1%
2,4,6	1,1,1	9.71	5.07	1.01
	1,2,3	5.59	3.33	0.86
	3,2,1	21.57	10.07	2.39

In order to explain this effect the test statistic K will be rewritten as a variance ratio VR. The Kruskal & Wallis test is equivalent to a one-way analysis of means on the ranks. We have:

$$VR = \frac{\sum_{i=1}^{k} n_i (\bar{R}_i - \bar{R})^2 / (k-1)}{\sum_{i=1}^{k} \sum_{j=1}^{n_i} (R_{ij} - \bar{R}_i)^2 / (N-k)}$$

The relationship between K and VR is:

$$VR = \frac{K(N-k)}{(k-1)(N-1-K)}$$

The denominator of VR can be rewritten as $\sum_{i=1}^{k}(n_i-1)s_i^2/(N-k)$, where s_i^2 is the sample variance of the ranks within the i-th sample. And here we have the explanation for the effect we saw in table 6. If the bigger variances happen to coincide with the bigger samples, the denominator will grow while the numerator will not be affected by this situation. Therefore the variance ratio VR will decrease. If we reverse the relation between K and VR we have:

$$K = \frac{(N-1)(k-1)VR}{(N-k)+(k-1)VR}$$

In this expression a decrease in VR will result in a decrease in K, because the denominator contains the term $(N-k)$ that is positive and unaffected by VR. Therefore the probability of rejecting a hypothesis will decrease, leaving the test conservative.

3.6. Adaptation to unequal variances

Since the Kruskal & Wallis test is not robust against variance hetero-geneity it seems attractive to replace the observations x_{ij} by $(x_{ij}-\text{med}(x))/\delta_i$, where med(x) is the pooled sample median and δ_i is a consistent estimate of the i-th scale parameter. Unfortunately Sen (1962) has already shown that such a test is not asymptotically distribution-free unless all the scale parameters are equal. However it is possible to construct a studentized quantile test that is based on the method of Mood & Brown (1950). Sen proposed the following test statistic:

$$S = 4[\sum_{i=1}^{k}\frac{1}{n_i}(m_i-\tfrac{1}{2}n_i)^2-\frac{1}{A}(\sum_{i=1}^{k}\frac{1}{\delta_i}(m_i-\tfrac{1}{2}n_i))^2]$$

Here m_i is the number of observations in the i-th sample not greater than med(x) and $A = \sum_{i=1}^{k}\frac{n_i}{\delta_i^2}$. Under mild conditions this statistic has asymptotically a χ^2 distribution with k - 1 degrees of freedom. For the estimates of the scale parameters Sen suggested:

$$\delta_i = (\frac{n_i}{2})^{-4} \sum_{j=1}^{en_i} (\frac{n_i}{2} - j)^3 z_{ij}$$

Here en_i denotes the entier of $\frac{1}{2} n_i$ and $z_{ij} = x_{i(n_i-j+1)} - x_{i(j)}$, where $x_{i(j)}$ is the j-th ordered value in the i-th sample. The efficiency of this estimate is 0.88 for the normal distribution with respect to the classical standard deviation. Since the asymptotic distribution of the test statistic does not depend on the choice of the scale parameter, and we want to use it here for normal distributions, Sen's test will also be considered in this study with the classical standard deviation.

Table 7: Sen's test with δ				
sample size	sigma	10%	5%	1%
4,4,4,4	1,1,1,1	5.72	4.88	0
	1,2,2,3	7.08	4.60	0.08
4,6,8,10	1,1,1,1	7.44	2.64	0.40
	1,2,2,3	5.92	3.00	0.36
	3,2,2,1	10.92	4.88	0.48
10,10,10,10	1,1,1,1	9.32	4.67	0.88
	1,2,2,3	9.24	5.20	0.44
4,4,4,4,4,4	1,1,1,1,1,1	8.64	3.36	0.04
	1,1,2,2,3,3	9.76	3.32	0.16
4,6,8,10,12,14	1,1,1,1,1,1	7.52	2.88	0.28
	1,1,2,2,3,3	5.72	3.20	0.32
	3,3,2,2,1,1	9.12	4.40	0.48
10,10,10,10,10,10	1,1,1,1,1,1	9.64	4.60	0.76
	1,1,2,2,3,3	9.16	4.52	0.36

From tables 7 and 8 we can see that this studentized modification of the Mood & Brown test gives better control over the chosen size than the Kruskal & Wallis test if the variances are unequal. It does not seem to matter very much whether the scale parameter for each group is estimated by δ_i or by the standard deviation s_i. Table 9 gives a

Table 8: Sen's test with s				
sample size	sigma	10%	5%	1%
4,4,4,4	1,1,1,1	5.96	4.68	0.04
	1,2,2,3	6.28	4.36	0.08
4,6,8,10	1,1,1,1	8.80	4.00	0.60
	1,2,2,3	8.84	3.72	0.48
	3,2,2,1	10.60	4.40	0.72
10,10,10,10	1,1,1,1	9.40	4.84	0.48
	1,2,2,3	10.52	4.80	0.76
4,4,4,4,4,4	1,1,1,1,1,1	8.08	3.96	0.72
	1,1,2,2,3,3	9.08	3.00	0.16
4,6,8,10,12,14	1,1,1,1,1,1	8.68	3.96	0.72
	1,1,2,2,3,3	7.64	3.92	0.56
	3,3,2,2,1,1	9.80	4.36	0.80
10,10,10,10,10,10	1,1,1,1,1,1	9.24	4.48	0.80
	1,1,2,2,3,3	9.76	4.56	0.72

summarized comparison between the influence of these estimates on the actual size of the test.

Table 9: Mean estimated size			
scale	nominal	mean	sigma
δ_i	10%	8.23	0.44
s_i	10%	8.76	0.37
δ_i	5%	4.01	0.27
s_i	5%	4.22	0.13
δ_i	1%	0.36	0.07
s_i	1%	0.55	0.07

In table 9 sigma denotes the estimated standard error of the mean. Every mean is based on 14 entries in table 7 or 8, and each of these entries is based on 2500 replications. It seems that the results for the standard deviation are slightly better than those for the scale parameter δ_i. If the nominal size is 5% or 10% the difference between the effects of the scale parameters is not very convincing. Only if the nominal size is 1% the choice of the standard deviation results in an improvement that exceeds the sum of the two estimated standard errors.

3.7. A comparison of powers

In table 10 the Kruskal & Wallis test with χ^2 is left out because the actual size exceeded the nominal size too much for some patters of sample sizes and variances. For a closer examination table 11 is produced. Here EMSV denotes that extreme means coincide with small variances, EMBV that extreme means coincide with big variances and EQV that all variances are equal. This distinction is made in order to compare the Kruskal & Wallis test with the second order James test. James uses the test statistic:

$$J = \sum_{i=1}^{k} w_i (\bar{x}_i - \bar{x})^2$$

Here $w_i = \dfrac{n_i}{s_i^2}$, $w = \sum_{i=1}^{k} w_i$ and $\bar{x} = \sum_{i=1}^{k} w_i \bar{x}_i / w$. This formula suggests that the power of the James test will be small if extreme means coincide with big variances. The Kruskal & Wallis test will not suffer from this problem because here the weights are simply n_i. If we compare for Sen's test his own scale parameter with the classical standard deviation we see that the latter gives slightly superior power. This is in accordance with the fact that the standard deviation is a more efficient estimate for the scale if the distribution is normal. However if we compare all the results for this studentized Mood & Brown test with the other two tests we see that the power is highly unsatisfactory. This can be partly explained by looking at the Asympotic Relative Efficiency of the Mood & Brown test relative to the Kruskal & Wallis test. Andrews (1954) found:

SS	mean	sigma	KW β	James2	Sen δ	Sen s
A	3,0,0,0	1,1,1,1	86.92	86.84	33.72	28.68
	5,0,0,$\frac{1}{2}$		99.64	99.64	27.96	36.24
	3,0,0,0	1,2,2,3	34.20	60.28	22.64	24.92
	0,0,0,3		25.36	22.72	13.56	12.64
	5,0,0,$\frac{1}{2}$		76.76	97.08	30.84	30.56
	$\frac{1}{2}$,0,0,5		56.00	43.72	18.72	18.92
B	3,0,0,0	1,1,1,1	88.32	92.88	12.68	16.12
	0,0,0,3		100	100	99.76	99.56
	3,0,0,0	1,2,2,3	25.08	86.96	8.48	13.48
	0,0,0,3		43.64	50.40	35.76	38.28
	5,0,0,$\frac{1}{2}$		72.04	99.88	12.60	18.68
	$\frac{1}{2}$,0,0,5		90.08	91.48	77.16	80.32
	3,0,0,0	3,2,2,1	26.84	24.12	10.32	9.24
	0,0,0,3		89.64	94.64	90.84	90.44
	5,0,0,$\frac{1}{2}$		62.56	51.64	16.16	16.44
C	3,0,0,0,0,0	1,1,1,1,1,1	66.08	91.60	9.20	13.96
		1,1,2,2,3,3	14.36	90.76	10.04	12.04
		3,3,2,2,1,1	24.12	23.96	9.20	8.08

Table 10: Estimated power with nominal size = 5%

SS	sample size
A	4,4,4,4
B	4,6,8,10
C	4,6,8,10,12,14

$$ARE_{MB,KW} = \frac{1}{3}[F'(M)/\int_{-\infty}^{\infty} F'(x)dF(x)]^2$$

Here M is the median of the distribution function F. If all the population variances are equal we have for the normal distribution $ARE_{MB,KW}$ = 2/3. And for this reason it is a pity that we cannot have a nonparametric studentized Kruskal & Wallis test.

Table 11: Summary of table 10				
category	KW β	James2	Sen δ	Sen s
EMSV	52.01	88.27	29.24	31.69
EMBV	46.94	44.00	25.90	26.27
EQV	88.19	94.19	36.66	38.91

If we compare the first two columns of table 11 we see that only in the EMSV case the second order test of James has considerably more power than the Kruskal & Wallis test. In the EMBV case the Kruskal & Wallis test has even slightly more power than the James test, and in the EQV case the superiority of the James test is only moderate. Can we conclude from this study that the Kruskal & Wallis test with the Beta approximation is a reasonable alternative for a test that is specially developed for normal populations with unequal variances? The answer can be yes, but with two serious restrictions:

1. If the sample sizes and the variances are unequal, and if the bigger variances coincide with the smaller samples, then the test will become progressive if the pattern is more extreme than those presented in the tables 1, 2 and 3. Roughly one might say that the maximum ratio of the standard deviations should not exceed 3.

2. A computer program for the Kruskal & Wallis test with Beta is much simpler than a program for the second order test of James. Therefore one might be tempted to use the former if the variances are not too different. It should be noted that by doing this one can lose a considerable amount of power, especially if extreme means coincide with small variances.

4. Nonparametric comparison of several mean values with adaptation to the tail-weights

4.1. Introduction

Several nonparametric tests exist for the hypothesis H_0 that k samples come from the same continuous distribution. Three of them will be considered in this study as a basis for an adaptive test with attractive properties for symmetric distributions with arbitrary tail-weights. The first one of these tests is the Van der Waerden test that uses the statistic:

$$Q_{VdW} = \frac{N-1}{\sum\limits_{i=1}^{N} [\Phi^{-1}(\frac{i}{N+1})]^2} \sum_{j=1}^{k} \frac{1}{n_j} [\sum_{i \in S_j} \Phi^{-1}(\frac{R_i}{N+1})]^2$$

Let $x_1, \ldots, x_N$ be a combination of the samples coming from k groups. S_j denotes the collection of indices in the j-th sample and n_j is the corresponding sample size. Φ is the standard normal distribution function. Nonparametric tests do not use all the information contained in the observations x_i but only their ranks R_i in the combined sample. The Kruskal & Wallis test was already mentioned in the third chapter. It uses the statistic:

$$Q_{KW} = \frac{12}{N(N+1)} \sum_{j=1}^{k} \frac{1}{n_j} [\sum_{i \in S_j} R_i - n_j \frac{N+1}{2}]^2$$

This formula is essentially the same as the one mentioned in the previous chapter. The third test originates from Mood & Brown (1950). It uses the statistic:

$$Q_{MB} = 4 \sum_{j=1}^{k} \frac{1}{n_j} [A_j - \frac{1}{2} n_j]^2$$

$$A_j = \sum_{i \in S_j} \frac{1}{2} [sign(R_i - \frac{1}{2}(N+1)) + 1]$$

Although the hypothesis under consideration is that all samples come from the same distribution, these tests are mostly used for the detection of a shift in the location parameters for distributions that are at least similar in shape and scale. The asymptotic distribution of the statistics under H_0 is χ^2 with k - 1 degrees of freedom. The behaviour of these tests if H_0 does not hold can differ considerably. For each test a distribution exists for which the power is asymptotically optimal (see table 1).

Table 1: Asymptotic optimality	
test	distribution
Kruskal & Wallis	logistic
Mood & Brown	double exponential
Van der Waerden	normal

It is possible to have a look at the data and then to decide which of these tests is the appropriate choice. The primary difference between the logistic, the double exponential and the normal distribution lies in their tails. If we call the tails of the logistic distribution moderate, it is natural to say that the normal distribution has light tails and that the tails of the double exponential distribution are heavy. So the principle of the adaptive test under consideration will be as follows: (1) get an impression of the tails from the samples, (2) determine whether they are light, moderate or heavy and (3) apply the appropriate test. Hajek and Sidak (1967) show that the information in the combined sample is independent of the ranks. Therefore the tails can be estimated, but it must be done from the observations without using information concerning the group to which they belong. If the location parameters are equal this is not a serious restriction. But if H_0 does not hold it is possible that the combined sample will suggest a tail-weight that differs considerably from the true value. One can put forward that this does not matter very much, because if the location parameters are so different that the combined sample does not represent the distribution of the separate samples, it is reasonable to suppose that any test will reject the hypothesis, so that it is not important whether the right one has been chosen. And if the location parameters differ only a little, then the tails will be estimated accurately, resulting in optimal power just where it is needed.

An adaptive nonparametric test where the above mentioned selection is based on the combined sample is not a rank test, but a permutation test. It would even be a test for which the probability of rejecting H_0 is equal to the chosen size α were it not that one usually is confronted with moderate sample sizes where the distribution of the test statistic can only be approximated by a χ^2-distribution. So if it is common practice to accept an approximation it is not unnatural to tolerate another deviation as long as it is small in comparison with the difference between the χ^2-distribution and the actual distribution of the test statistic for moderate samples. A kind of cheating that would introduce an error is the following: compute Q_{KW}, Q_{MB} and Q_{VdW} and then compare the maximum of these values with the critical value based on the χ^2 approximation. Such a strategy will certainly result in a powerful test, but it is something no serious statistician would consider because the probability of rejecting H_0 when true will exceed the chosen size α.

There is however a kind of "moderate cheating" that will be considered in this study. In the selection scheme the tails will be estimated from the combined sample, but also from an artificial sample that is based on the original observations after a shift to give every group the same location parameter. It is reasonable to suppose that this shift will result in better estimates for the tails. In a simulation study we will examine this, and an attempt will be presented to quantify the error that is introduced by this incorrect use of information.

4.2. Asymptotic relative efficiency

Application of an adaptive test that is based on the methods of Van der Waerden, Kruskal & Wallis and Mood & Brown is only worthwhile if the powers of these separate tests are very different for the distributions under consideration. An attractive criterion for comparing the powers is the Asymptotic Relative Efficiency (ARE) that is also known as the Pitman efficiency. Let A and B be tests and let a and b be the corresponding number of observations involved. For some chosen size α both tests are used for the same hypothesis H_0 against a class of alternatives H_c. Then $ARE_{A,B}$ is defined as the asymptotic value of $\dfrac{b}{a}$ when a varies such that the powers are (and remain) equal while $b \to \infty$ and $H_c \to H_0$.

Andrews (1954) gives a formula for the ARE of the Mood & Brown test relative to the Kruskal & Wallis test:

$$ARE_{MB,KW} = \frac{1}{3}[F'(M)/\int_{-\infty}^{\infty} F'(x)dF(x)]^2$$

Here M is the median of F. A more general formula has been given by Puri (1964) that can be used to compare any pair of nonparametric k-sample tests for some chosen distribution. This could be used to compute the other asymptotic relative efficiencies, but in this study they are found in a different way. Terry and Hoeffding proposed a test that is very similar to the Van der Waerden test and that has the same asymptotic relative efficiencies [Bradley (1968)]. Hodges and Lehman (1961) examined the two-sample situation for $ARE_{TH,W}$ (W stands for Wilcoxon which is the Kruskal & Wallis test for two samples). With these results it is possible to construct table 2.

Table 2: Asymptotic Relative Efficiency			
distribution	$ARE_{VdW,KW}$	$ARE_{VdW,MB}$	$ARE_{KW,MB}$
normal	$\dfrac{\pi}{3}$	$\dfrac{\pi}{2}$	$\dfrac{3}{2}$
logistic	$\dfrac{3}{\pi}$	$\dfrac{4}{\pi}$	$\dfrac{4}{3}$
double exponential	$\dfrac{8}{3\pi}$	$\dfrac{2}{\pi}$	$\dfrac{3}{4}$

Some of the entries in table 2 differ seriously from 1. This suggests that an adaptive test that is based on the methods by Van der Waerden, Kruskal & Wallis and Mood & Brown will have good power for a large class of symmetric distributions with arbitrary tail-weights. For this it will be necessary to have an accurate method to estimate the distribution from the samples. Suppose the estimation is done with the combined sample while the location parameters are unequal. If the data come from a normal distribution the combined sample will look flatter so that it can be classified as a double exponential distribution. This will result in a considerable loss of power relative to the correct selection. Centralisation on the location parameters can prevent this situation from happening.

4.3. Criteria for selecting the test

In a simulation study samples were generated from normal, logistic and double exponential distributions [see appendix 4]. This study was restricted to the case of 4 samples, each coming from the same (but shifted) distribution. Several criteria for selecting the test were considered. The first was the sample kurtosis of the combined sample:

$$K = \frac{\sum\limits_{i=1}^{N}(x_i - \bar{x})^4/N}{[\sum\limits_{i=1}^{N}(x_i - \bar{x})^2/N]^2} - 3$$

The kurtoses for the distributions under consideration are well known (see table 3). To use the kurtosis as a criterion for selecting the test it was necessary to choose boundary values for K somewhere between the kurtoses for the distributions under consideration. In the absence of a better idea the midpoints were chosen. Table 4 shows how K is tried in the adaptive test. This use of K as a method to recognise the normal, logistic and double exponential distribution proved to be very disappointing. The second idea was to shift the samples to make the means equal and to compute K for the combination of these shifted samples. This resulted in an improvement but the fraction of correct classifications was still not satisfactory. Another improvement was achieved by a centralisation on the medians instead of the means. This was tried because the experiment involved the double exponential distribution with very heavy tails. Unfortunately also this approach did not prove to be a succes. The last attempt with the kurtosis was based

Table 3: Kurtosis		
distribution	K	criterion
normal	0	
		0.6
logistic	1.2	
		2.1
double exponential	3	

Table 4: Selection on K	
kurtosis	test
$K < 0.6$	Van der Waerden
$0.6 \leqslant K < 2.1$	Kruskal & Wallis
$2.1 \leqslant K$	Mood & Brown

on the weighted mean of the values K_i for the separate samples. This proved to be similar to centralisation on the means.

So the kurtosis as a criterion for selecting the test had to be rejected. How is it possible that this statistic that is often referred to as a measure of flatness can not be used as an indicator for three distributions that are so different in their tail-weights? Mood, Graybill and Boes (1963) mention that the kurtosis can be used to measure the peakedness or flatness of a density, but mostly around the center. It seems that they are right; it is certainly impossible to get much information about the tails from the kurtosis.

This disappointment made it necessary to look for others measures of tail-weight and two were found. Uthoff (1970 and 1973) suggested:

$$U = \frac{Z_N - Z_1}{2 \sum_{i=1}^{N} |Z_i - med_i(Z_i)| / N}$$

Here $Z_1, \dots, Z_N$ is the ordered sample. Uthoff has shown that the best location and scale invariant test of an underlying uniform distribution against the double exponential is based on a ratio to which U is an approximation. Since the uniform distribution has lighter tails (if one may even speak of them) than the normal distribution, this statistic seems a promising candidate. Hogg, Fisher and Randles (1975) suggested using:

$$Q = \frac{10(U_{.05} - L_{.05})}{U_{.5} - L_{.5}}$$

They tried this statistic in a similar study as the present one, where they also included a measure of skewness, but their objective was restricted to the construction of a two-sample adaptive distribution-free test. $U_{.05}$ denotes the sum of the upper 5% of the observations. If N is not a multiple of 20 then one observation is only fractionally included. The other parts of this formula have a similar meaning, where L stands for lower. It turns out that U and Q are very similar and 10U and Q are even identical if N does not exceed 20. The use of Q as a criterion for selecting the test is given in tables 5 and 6.

Table 5: Criterion Q		
distribution	Q	criterion
normal	2.58	
		2.72
logistic	2.86	
		3.08
double exponential	3.30	

Table 6: Selection on Q	
$Q < 2.72$	Van der Waerden
$2.72 \leqslant Q < 3.08$	Kruskal & Wallis
$3.08 \leqslant Q$	Mood & Brown

The derivation of the population values of Q for the normal, logistic and double exponential distribution is given in appendix 5. For the criterion the midpoints between these population values were chosen.

Two adaptive tests were considered for this selection scheme. In the coming sections A-P will denote the test where the selection is not preceded by centralisation so that Q is computed for the combined sample, resulting in a pure adaptive nonparametric test where the only source for a difference between the nominal size and the actual probability of a rejection under the hypothesis of equal population means comes from using the χ^2 approximation. As an alternative A-C will also be considered where the computation of Q is preceded by centralisation on the medians. So we have:

A-P: A Pure Adaptive test

A-C: An Adaptive test with Centralisation (or Cheating)

4.4. The adaptive tests under the null hypothesis

In a simulation study the probability of a rejection under H_0 is examined. For 4 groups and 5, 15 and 60 observations for each group the actual percentage of rejections is estimated. In table 7, 9 and 11 every entry is based on 2500 replications. The actual size was chosen as 5%, so that the standard error for the estimated sizes was 0.436%. Not only the normal, logistic and double exponential distributions were used in this simulation, but also the uniform distribution with lighter tails than the normal, and the Cauchy distribution with heavier tails than the double exponential [see appendix 4].

Table 7: Estimated size, $n_i = 5$					
distribution	K&W	M&B	VdW	A-P	A-C
uniform	3.92	4.92	3.72	3.72	3.72
normal	3.72	5.04	3.40	3.48	3.52
logistic	3.80	4.84	3.48	3.92	4.28
double exponential	4.16	4.92	3.88	4.24	4.44
Cauchy	3.88	4.52	3.52	4.40	4.36

As the sample size tends to infinity the values of Q for the uniform and the Cauchy distribution are respectively 1.9 and 10 [see appendix 5]. The probability that the appropriate test is selected is not

Table 8: Selected tests, $n_i = 5$						
	A–P			A–C		
distribution	VdW	K&W	M&B	VdW	K&W	M&B
uniform	2494	6		2358	126	16
normal	1927	407	166	1777	474	249
logistic	1470	594	436	1351	621	528
double exp	893	649	958	829	620	1051
Cauchy	90	163	2247	84	150	2266

Table 9: Estimated size, $n_i = 15$					
distribution	K&W	M&B	VdW	A–P	A–C
uniform	4.48	3.44	4.56	4.56	4.56
normal	4.92	4.00	5.32	5.24	5.40
logistic	4.76	4.20	4.92	4.92	4.96
double exponential	4.92	4.24	4.72	4.44	4.56
Cauchy	5.00	4.44	4.72	4.44	4.44

Table 10: Selected tests, $n_i = 15$						
	A–P			A–C		
distribution	VdW	K&W	M&B	VdW	K&W	M&B
uniform	2500			2483	17	
normal	1997	469	34	1902	552	46
logistic	1062	1049	389	997	1062	441
double exp	200	803	1497	182	782	1536
Cauchy		1	2499			2500

everywhere satisfactory. For the uniform, normal, double exponential and Cauchy distribution the test with the highest power was selected in most cases for every sample size and both adaptive tests. But for the logistic distribution with $N_i = 5$ both A-P and A-C selected the Van

Table 11: Estimated size, $n_i = 60$					
distribution	K&W	M&B	VdW	A-P	A-C
uniform	4.48	4.24	4.72	4.72	4.72
normal	5.44	5.52	5.20	5.32	5.32
logistic	5.32	5.28	5.36	5.28	5.40
double exponential	5.12	4.64	5.04	4.76	4.72
Cauchy	5.68	5.32	5.52	5.32	5.32

Table 12: Selected tests, $n_i = 60$						
	A-P			A-C		
distribution	VdW	K&W	M&B	VdW	K&W	M&B
uniform	2500			2500		
normal	2224	276		2188	312	
logistic	468	1904	128	447	1911	142
double exp	1	319	2180	1	313	2186
Cauchy			2500			2500

der Waerden test more often than the Kruskal & Wallis test. This strange effect is still visible in the results for $n_i = 15$ and it vanishes almost completely for $n_i = 60$.

In order to find the origin of this effect the following experiment was carried out. Since there were 4 groups with 5, 15 or 60 observations A-P selected the test on the value of Q for a sample of 20, 60 or 240 random numbers from the chosen distribution. For the logistic distribution 1000 values of Q were computed with each of these sample sizes. Histograms were plotted and these demonstrated that the distribution Q_{20} is strongly skewed, the distribution of Q_{60} is somewhat skewed and the distribution of Q_{240} is nearly symmetric. The results can be summarized by the minimum, modus and maximum of these estimated distributions of Q (see table 13), where the extremes are added to give an indication of the tails. Table 13 explains the unsatisfactory selection for small samples if the distribution is logistic. For

Table 13: Skewness of Q (logistic distribution)			
sample size	minimum	modus	maximum
20	1.59	2.55	4.79
60	2.05	2.76	4.06
240	2.48	2.84	3.39

combined samples of 20 observations the modus of Q is even slightly smaller than the expectation for the normal distribution. So it is clear that the selection scheme can be improved by taking the combined sample size into account. The gain in power can only be very moderate, because the ARE of the Van der Waerden test relative to the Kruskal & Wallis test is $\frac{3}{\pi}$ for the logistic distribution. If one takes N into account A-P will still be a pure nonparametric adaptive test, because the information contained in the sample size is already present before the experiment is carried out. A study on such an adaptive scheme is started while this is written, so it can not be presented here. It may result in a very small gain concerning the power, but it is unreasonable to expect much of it.

Since the location parameters were equal in this simulation the combined sample should represent the underlying distribution better than the result of a centralization on the medians. In table 14 the performance of the selection methods in A-P and A-C is compared. In addition to the criteria given in table 5 and 6 it is clear that the uniform distribution should select the Van der Waerden test and that for the Cauchy distribution the Mood & Brown test would be the best choice. For both adaptive tests and the three sample sizes under consideration the number of correct selections is presented. In the case of a misclassification a distinction is made between a neighbouring test and the selection of the opposite extreme (Van der Waerden when it should be Mood & Brown and vice versa). For both tests the probability of a correct selection increases rapidly with the sample size. As was to be expected the selection scheme of A-P is better under H_0 than that of A-C. The difference is noticable if $n_i = 5$ and it nearly vanishes if $n_i = 60$.

Table 14: Comparison of selection schemes under H_0				
test	sample size	correct	neighbour	opposite
A-P	5	8220	3131	1149
	15	9542	2724	234
	60	11308	1191	1
A-C	5	8073	3249	1178
	15	9483	2789	228
	60	11285	1214	1

The test A-C with centralisation on the medians is not a pure non-parametric adaptive test, because it uses information that is not contained in the ranks. The worst that could happen as a result of this is that the probability of a rejection under H_0 exceeds the chosen size α. To examine this table 15 is produced, where the results for all the sample sizes are combined. The standard error of the estimated sizes is 0.436%. Let d be the actual percentage of rejections under H_0 minus the nominal size and this divided by the standard deviation. The test will seem accurate concerning the size if $-2 \leqslant d < 2$, conservative if $d < -2$ and progressive if $2 \leqslant d$. These categories are separated by double lines. Because the Kruskal & Wallis, Van der Waerden and Mood & Brown tests are somewhat conservative for small samples if the χ^2 approximation is used, it is not amazing that both adaptive tests show the same inclination. In table 15 both A-P and A-C never showed a size that exceeded the nominal value by more than one standard deviation. In this respect they seem even better than the original tests, where this value was exceeded by all three of them. So in this stage of the study there seems to be no reason to distrust A-C, and if its power should prove to be much better than that of A-P, then the use of a centralization in the selection scheme could be recommended.

	K&W	M&B	VdW	A-P	A-C
Table 15: Summary of tables 7, 9 and 11					
$d < -3$		1	3	1	1
$-3 \leqslant d < -2$	4	1	2	2	1
$-2 \leqslant d < -1$	3	5	1	5	6
$-1 \leqslant d < 1$	6	7	8	7	7
$1 \leqslant d < 2$	2	1	1		
$2 \leqslant d < 3$					
$3 \leqslant d$					

4.5. A comparison of powers

distribution	K&W	M&B	VdW	A-P	A-C
Table 16: Estimated power, $n_i = 15$ Location: 0, 0.15, 0.3, 1.05					
uniform	62.3	25.0	73.0	73.0	73.0
normal	70.7	43.3	70.7	70.3	71.0
logistic	26.3	15.0	25.3	24.0	25.3
double exponential	51.7	45.7	47.7	48.0	50.3
Cauchy	20.0	23.3	16.7	23.3	23.3

The powers of the tests under consideration are estimated by the number of rejections from 300 replications. The results are given as percentages. Samples are considered with 15, 40 and 65 observations. In practical analysis of means situations one is not often confronted with samples containing more than 40 observations. A sample size of 65 is only included in the analysis because with the other two values it will be possible to see the performance of the selection schemes of A-P and A-C as a function of the sample size. Eight different sets of location parameters were tried, but since the results of them proved to be very similar, only two sets are presented in the tables. The logistic, normal, double exponential and Cauchy distribution have a scale

Table 17: Selected tests, $n_i = 15$ Location: 0, 0.15, 0.3, 1.05						
	A-P			A-C		
distribution	VdW	K&W	M&B	VdW	K&W	M&B
uniform	300			300		
normal	228	64	8	216	77	7
logistic	126	139	35	109	152	39
double exp	51	127	122	28	97	175
Cauchy		1	299		1	299

Table 18: Estimated power, $n_i = 40$ Location: 0, 0.15, 0.3, 1.05					
distribution	K&W	M&B	VdW	A-P	A-C
uniform	98.0	69.7	99.3	99.3	99.3
normal	100	95.3	100	100	100
logistic	68.7	55.3	69.0	65.7	66.7
double exponential	94.3	92.7	90.3	93.0	93.3
Cauchy	56.0	67.7	44.3	67.7	67.7

parameter. For all these parameters the value 1 was chosen. In order to get a uniform distribution with unit variance the range of this distribution was chosen as $\sqrt{12}$. If the location parameters are unequal the combined sample will suggest a flatter density than the actual distribution. Centralization can result in an improvement here, especially if the location parameters are very different. In this simulation the shifts were chosen such that for sample size 65 at least one entry in the table for the estimated power was 100%. This value was not permitted to occur for every entry in a row, because this would not yield any information concerning the relative powers. These restrictions resulted in moderate shifts and a simulation was needed to decide whether centralization improves the probability of a correct selection if the location parameters differ only as little as presented in the tables. In table

Table 19: Selected tests, $n_i = 40$ Location: 0, 0.15, 0.3, 1.05						
	A-P			A-C		
distribution	VdW	K&W	M&B	VdW	K&W	M&B
uniform	300			300		
normal	259	41		252	47	1
logistic	106	177	17	80	198	22
double exp	1	125	174	3	66	231
Cauchy			300			300

Table 20: Estimated power, $n_i = 65$ Location: 0, 0.15, 0.3, 1.05					
distribution	K&W	M&B	VdW	A-P	A-C
uniform	100	89.0	100	100	100
normal	100	99.7	100	100	100
logistic	92.0	77.3	89.7	90.7	91.7
double exponential	99.7	99.0	99.7	99.3	99.3
Cauchy	80.7	89.7	70.3	89.7	89.7

Table 21: Selected tests, $n_i = 65$ Location: 0, 0.15, 0.3, 1.05						
	A-P			A-C		
distribution	VdW	K&W	M&B	VdW	K&W	M&B
uniform	300			300		
normal	282	18		274	26	
logistic	67	220	13	46	238	16
double exp		92	208		40	260
Cauchy			300			300

Table 22: Estimated power, $n_i = 15$
Location: 0, 0.1, 0.5, 0.9

distribution	K&W	M&B	VdW	A-P	A-C
uniform	51.0	18.7	62.3	62.3	62.3
normal	53.7	32.0	55.7	55.0	55.3
logistic	23.3	15.3	24.0	22.3	22.0
double exponential	44.3	39.0	41.0	41.3	43.3
Cauchy	15.7	15.7	13.0	15.7	15.7

Table 23: Selected tests, $n_i = 15$
Location: 0, 0.1, 0.5, 0.9

distribution	A-P			A-C		
	VdW	K&W	M&B	VdW	K&W	M&B
uniform	300			297	3	
normal	242	51	7	227	62	11
logistic	122	140	38	113	135	52
double exp	49	110	141	31	91	178
Cauchy		1	299			300

Table 24: Estimated power, $n_i = 40$
Location: 0, 0.1, 0.5, 0.9

distribution	K&W	M&B	VdW	A-P	A-C
uniform	94.3	51.7	99.0	99.0	99.0
normal	97.0	88.3	97.3	97.3	97.3
logistic	56.3	41.3	52.0	53.0	54.3
double exponential	88.3	85.7	81.3	88.0	88.0
Cauchy	47.3	57.0	33.3	57.0	57.0

28 the performance of the selection rules of A-P and A-C are presented. Just like in table 14 a distinction is made between the selection of a neighbouring test and the selection of an opposite one (Van der Waerden when it should be Mood & Brown and vice versa). For both rules the probability of a correct selection increases with the sample size. We saw already that under H_0 it is better not to centralize on the medians. But here, where the location parameters are different, it can be seen that for every sample size the selection rule of A-C performs better than that of A-P. This is not only true for the combination of all the results in this section as presented in table 28, but also for each of the separate alternatives concerning the location parameters.

Table 25: Selected tests, n_i = 40 Location: 0, 0.1, 0.5, 0.9						
	A-P			A-C		
distribution	VdW	K&W	M&B	VdW	K&W	M&B
uniform	300			300		
normal	264	36		254	46	
logistic	78	195	27	76	201	23
double exp	3	117	180		78	222
Cauchy			300			300

Table 26: Estimated power, n_i = 65 Location: 0, 0.1, 0.5, 0.9					
distribution	K&W	M&B	VdW	A-P	A-C
uniform	99.0	78.7	100	100	100
normal	100	97.7	100	100	100
logistic	79.7	67.7	80.8	79.3	80.0
double exponential	98.7	99.0	97.3	99.0	99.3
Cauchy	75.0	85.0	59.3	85.0	85.0

In table 29 the powers of all tests considered are estimated as the

Table 27: Selected tests, $n_i = 65$ Location: 0, 0.1, 0.5, 0.9						
	A-P			A-C		
distribution	VdW	K&W	M&B	VdW	K&W	M&B
uniform	300			300		
normal	272	28		260	40	
logistic	62	229	9	43	245	12
double exp		101	199		51	249
Cauchy			300			300

percentage of rejections for all situations in this section together. This means that a mixture with equal occurences from the uniform, normal, logistic, double exponential and Cauchy distribution is submitted to the analysis. It can be seen that for every sample size the adaptive tests have more power than the separate tests. A-C is always better than A-P, but the difference is only marginal.

Table 28: Comparison of selection schemes Location parameters are unequal				
test	sample size	correct	neighbour	opposite
A-P	15	2210	675	115
	40	2449	547	4
	65	2610	390	
A-C	15	2279	644	77
	40	2558	438	4
	65	2726	274	

The final conclusions of this study are a bit disappointing. If one is interested in the comparison of several mean values, and the only thing that is known about the underlying distribution is that it is symmetric, one can consider to use an adaptive test like A-P or A-C. But in the simulation presented here the gain in power relative to the Kruskal & Wallis test (which is optimal for the middle range of Q and

Table 29: Comparison of powers Mixture of 5 distributions					
sample size	K&W	M&B	VdW	A-P	A-C
15	41.90	27.63	42.93	43.53	44.17
40	80.03	70.47	76.60	82.00	82.27
65	92.47	88.27	89.63	94.30	94.50

therefore never the worst choice) is only moderate. Asymptotically both adaptive tests are superior for a mixture of symmetric distributions as described in this study. And the element of cheating in A-C will disappear as the sample size increases. But for finite samples the results are disappointing. This can be partly explained by the observation that for sample sizes 15 and 40 the Kruskal & Wallis test demonstrates more power for the double exponential distribution than the Mood & Brown test that is asymptotically optimal for this distribution. Only for samples with 65 observations the asymptotical superiority of the Mood & Brown test becomes visible in table 26, but in table 20 for the same sample size the Kruskal & Wallis test is still slightly superior for the double exponential distribution. In this study only two shifts of the location parameters were presented out of the total of eight that were generated. There were situations in the other six where the Mood & Brown test showed more power for the double exponential distribution than the Kruskal & Wallis test for samples with 40 observations. But for smaller samples the Mood & Brown test was always inferior.

So for small samples the correct recognition of a double exponential distribution leads to a loss of power in the adaptive tests relative to the Kruskal & Wallis test. This, as well as the skewed distribution of Q for the logistic distribution (see table 13), leads to the conclusion that a better adaptive test can be constructed by taking the sample size into account in the selection scheme. These improvements are the topic of a study that has just started and therefore the results will not be presented here. The expected outcome of this study is not a considerable gain in power, as can be concluded from the tables in this section. But for the tool-forger every small improvement can be tempting, even if it has not much practical value.

For symmetric distributions the Kruskal & Wallis test is never a very bad choice. It is possible to get a bit more power by using an adaptive test, but the gain is little in comparison with the extra programming effort. The selection scheme in this study can be improved by taking the sample size into account, but also this can only result in a very moderate gain in power.

5. Comparison of several mean values in the presence of outliers

5.1. Introduction

The model in classical one-way analysis of means is $y_{ij} = \mu_i + e_{ij}$ where the errors e_{ij} are supposed to be independently distributed as $N(0,\sigma^2)$ with unknown population variance σ^2. The index i denotes the group-number (i = 1 , ... , k) and j identifies the elements within the groups (j = 1 , ... , n_i). The hypothesis of interest is H_0: $\mu_1 = ... = \mu_k$. According to the above conditions, this hypothesis can be tested with:

$$ F = \frac{\sum\limits_{i=1}^{k} n_i (\bar{y}_i - \bar{y})^2 / (k-1)}{\sum\limits_{i=1}^{k} \sum\limits_{j=1}^{n_i} (y_{ij} - \bar{y}_i)^2 / (N-k)} $$

Here $N = \sum\limits_{i=1}^{k} n_i$. $\bar{y}_i$ is the sample mean within the i-th group and $\bar{y}$ is the overall sample mean. This statistic has under H_0 an F-distribution with k - 1 and N - k degrees of freedom.

For contaminated normal data we consider the following modification: with (small) probability ϵ the distribution becomes $e_{ij} \simeq N(0,\theta\sigma^2)$, where $\theta >> 1$, and with probability 1-ϵ the distribution remains $N(0,\sigma^2)$. This contamination is symmetric; in the asymmetric case, multiplication by θ is performed on the positive errors only, with probability 2ϵ. In both cases, the expected fraction of outliers is ϵ.

Classical one-way analysis of means is not designed for contaminated normal data. Using this test here might result in a probability of rejecting H_0 when true that differs from the chosen size α, or in a serious loss of power. Suppose for example that the data represent the heights of people, coming from different groups. Suppose the analist works at a computer-terminal and he enters the data in meters with two decimals. But sometimes, though not often, he can forget to enter the decimal point. Here we have a small value of ϵ, the multiplication factor θ is considerably bigger than 1, and the contamination is one-sided.

What will happen to the statistic F? The overall sample mean $\bar{y}$ will increase as well as one or more of the group means. As a consequence the numerator of the statistic will increase, but also the denominator. So at first sight it seems difficult to predict what will happen to F. More attention to this will be given further in this chapter. Some alternatives will be presented that seem more robust in these respects. A comparative study concerning the size and power of all the tests under consideration will be given, where the effect of symmetric and one-sided contamination is demonstrated by simulation.

5.2. Nonparametric analysis of means

In a nonparametric test the hypothesis is not the same as in the previous section, but it can be expressed as "all samples come from the same continuous distribution". Nonparametric analysis of means has very little power in the comparison of shapes, so it can only be used to test the equality of location parameters. The density in case of symmetric contamination is given by:

$$f(x) = \epsilon \frac{1}{\sigma\sqrt{\theta 2\pi}} \exp[-\frac{x^2}{2\theta\sigma^2}] + (1-\epsilon)\frac{1}{\sigma\sqrt{2\pi}}\exp[-\frac{x^2}{2\sigma^2}]$$

and this represents a continuous distribution. Therefore the application of nonparametric analysis of means is permitted. It is easily seen that this also holds for one-sided contamination.

Several nonparametric tests are available, but here we will only use the Van der Waerden (1952) test. This test is based on the following statistic:

$$Q = \frac{N-1}{\sum_{g=1}^{N}[\Phi^{-1}(\frac{g}{N+1})]^2} \sum_{i=1}^{k}\frac{1}{n_i}[\sum_{g \in S_i}\Phi^{-1}(\frac{R_g}{N+1})]^2$$

Here $y_1, \ldots, y_N$ represents the combined sample, where the groups are represented by sets of indices S_i for i = 1, ... , k. R_g is the rank of y_g and Φ denotes the standard normal distribution function. Q is asymptotically distributed as χ^2 with k - 1 degrees of freedom. The reason for choosing the Van der Waerden test from the existing collection of methods for nonparametric analysis of means, lies in the fact that this is the only test that has for $\epsilon = 0$ asymptotically the same efficiency as the classical test [Hajek (1969)]. By using this nonparametric method one is insured against the possible presence of outliers, and the premium one has to pay is the loss of power for small samples. For k = 2 this loss has already been shown to be moderate [Van der Laan and Oosterhoff (1967)] and further in this chapter we will see that this is also true for more than two samples. If there are many outliers the tests by Mood & Brown or Kruskal & Wallis are better choices [Hampel, Ronchetti, Rousseeuw and Stahel (1986)]. But this situation will not be considered in this chapter.

5.3. Winsorizing and trimming

Applications of these methods to the t-test for two samples have been published already [Fung and Rahman (1980), Yuen and Dixon (1973)]. The t-test uses the statistic:

$$ t = \frac{\bar{y}_1 - \bar{y}_2}{\sqrt{(SS_1 + SS_2)/(n_1 + n_2 - 2)}\sqrt{1/n_1 + 1/n_2}} $$

$$ \text{with } SS_i = \sum_{j=1}^{n_i} (y_{ij} - \bar{y}_i)^2 $$

Under the hypothesis of equal population means this test statistic follows a t-distribution with N-2 degrees of freedom if $\epsilon = 0$. This method is equivalent to classical one-way analysis of means for k = 2 ($t^2 = F$ and for the critical values the same relation holds: $t_\nu^2 \simeq F_\nu^1$).

Fung and Rahman (1980) Winsorized the t-test in an attempt to make it robust against the presence of outliers. This is done as follows: let a_1, ... , a_n be an ordered sample. Then the mean and sum of squares of this sample, after two-sided Winsorizing with parameter g, are defined as:

$$\bar{a}_{wg} = \frac{1}{n}[(g+1)a_{g+1} + a_{g+2} + \ldots + a_{n-g-1} + (g+1)a_{n-g}]$$

$$SS_{wg} = (g+1)(a_{g+1} - \bar{a}_{wg})^2 + (a_{g+2} - \bar{a}_{wg})^2 + \ldots$$
$$+ (a_{n-g-1} - \bar{a}_{wg})^2 + (g+1)(a_{n-g} - \bar{a}_{wg})^2$$

The number of relevant observations hereby reduces to h = n-2g. The value of g should be chosen such that it is reasonable to suppose that all the outliers will be contained in the tails of the samples, so that their values become irrelevant. Application of this technique to the t-test gives the following formula:

$$t_{wg} = \frac{\bar{y}_{1wg} - \bar{y}_{2wg}}{\sqrt{(SS_{1wg} + SS_{2wg})/(h_1 + h_2 - 2)}\sqrt{1/h_1 + 1/h_2}}$$

This statistic approximately follows a t-distribution with $h_1 + h_2 - 2$ degrees of freedom. Fung and Rahman used n_i instead of h_i under the second square-root sign, but that appears to have been a typing error as can be concluded from a study by Yuen and Dixon (1973) on which they based their approach.

Winsorizing means replacing the tail-elements by the most extreme elements that are not considered to belong to the tails. Trimming is a different technique in which the tail-elements are simply deleted. Yuen and Dixon examined the behaviour of the trimmed t-test, where the numerator is based on trimmed means, but the denominator still contains Winsorized sums of squares. In a simulation study with samples containing at least 10 observations each, both methods show the same qualities: The probability of rejecting H_0 when true is almost equal to the chosen size, and the power for normal distributions is only slightly below that of the classical t-test for moderate values of g. For distributions with heavier tails the Winsorized and trimmed t-tests are even more powerful than the classical t-test for moderate values of g [Fung and Rahman (1980)].

Therefore it could be attractive to apply these techniques to classical one-way anova, which is the natural generalisation of the t-test for more than two samples. The Winsorized F-statistic is given by:

$$F_{wg} = \frac{\sum_{i=1}^{k} h_i (\bar{y}_{iwg} - \bar{y}_{wg})^2 / (k-1)}{\sum_{i=1}^{k} SS_{iwg} / (H-k)}$$

Here $\bar{y}_{wg} = \sum_{i=1}^{k} h_i \bar{y}_{iwg} / H$ and $H = \sum_{i=1}^{k} h_i$. For the trimmed F-statistic F_{tg} only the numerator is modified: the Winsorized means are replaced by trimmed means $\bar{y}_{itg}$ and the trimmed overall sample mean is given by $\bar{y}_{tg} = \sum_{i=1}^{k} h_i \bar{y}_{itg} / H$. It is assumed that both F_{wg} and F_{tg} are approximately distributed as an F-distribution with k-1 and H-k degrees of freedom. In a previous simulation [Dijkstra (1986)] it was found that the probability of rejecting H_0 when true differs too much from the chosen size for Winsorized analysis of means. But after correction of the above mentioned typing error in the paper by Fung and Rahman the behaviour of these tests improved remarkably as will be shown later in this chapter.

5.4. Outlier resistant regression

The model for analysis of means can be rewritten as a regression model:

$$y = \beta_1 x_1 + \ldots + \beta_k x_k + e$$

The observations are represented by y and for every observation the group to which it belongs is identified by the dummy-variables $x_1, \ldots, x_k$. This can be done as follows: $x_i = 1$ if y belongs to group i and otherwise $x_i = 0$. If the errors were independently distributed as $N(0,\sigma^2)$ then testing: $H_0: \beta_1 = \ldots = \beta_k$ would be equivalent to testing $H_0: \mu_1 = \ldots = \mu_k$ in the model for classical one-way analysis of means. The values of F and the corresponding numbers of degrees of freedom would be the same.

Several methods for dealing with outliers in regression have already been published. Huber (1973) suggested a method with attractive properties that can be applied to the analysis of means problem in this study.

The objective of classical regression is to minimize $\sum_{i=1}^{N}(y_i-x_i\beta)^2$ as a function of $\beta=(\beta_1,\dots,\beta_k)$. Here $x_i=(x_{i1},\dots,x_{ik})^T$. It can easily be understood that outliers in y will have considerable influence on the estimation of β, because classical regression will square their residuals. A more robust method minimizes another objective:

$$M(\beta)=\sum_{i=1}^{N}\rho(\frac{y_i-x_i\beta}{\sigma})$$

In the classical case $\rho(r)=r^2$, but in robust regression one chooses a function that limits the influence of extreme residuals. Holland and Welsch (1977) mention eight different functions ρ with this desirable property. The objective $M(\beta)$ will be at its minimum if:

$$\sum_{i=1}^{N}x_{ij}\,\Psi(\frac{y_i-x_i\beta}{\sigma})=0$$

for $j=1,\dots,k$ and $\Psi(r)=\dfrac{d\,\rho(r)}{dr}$. Several iterative methods for solving these equations can be considered. Initial estimates for $\beta_1,\dots,\beta_k$ can be obtained by ordinairy least squares, whereafter σ can be estimated as:

$$\hat{\sigma}=1.4826[med_j\,|(y_j-x_j\beta)-med_i\,(y_i-x_i\beta)|\,]$$

Here med_i denotes the median over the index i. The factor 1.4826 makes this an approximately unbiased estimate of the standard deviation in the case of normal errors. Without restrictions on the weight function, convergence cannot in general be guaranteed if the estimation of σ is part of the iteration. Huber (1973) found a ρ that allows iteratively re-estimating of σ:

$$\rho(r)=\frac{r^2}{2}\text{ for }|r|\leqslant H$$

$$\rho(r) = H|r| - \frac{H^2}{2} \text{ for } |r| > H$$

The sensitivity to outliers depends on the value of H. For H = 1.345 the efficiency is 95% for normal distributions. If the absolute value of a standardised residual exceeds H, its influence becomes linear instead of quadratic. Although Huber's ρ does not yield an extremely robust estimate (some authors prefer a ρ that becomes a constant for large values of $|r|$), this method is a considerable improvement on ordinary least squares in the presence of outliers. In this case Newton's method yields a very efficient algorithm, because Ψ is a broken linear function.

For the construction of an outlier-resistant analysis of means procedure we consider the above mentioned robust regression with Huber's ρ and H = 1.345. This approach results in fitted values $\hat{y}_i$ and an estimate $\hat{\sigma}$ for σ. Huber (1981) suggested a test for the hypothesis of equal population means that uses these estimates. His suggestion is the topic of the next section.

5.5. Huber's method

In the classical situation (without outliers) the test statistic for $H_0: \mu_1 = \dots = \mu_k$ is:

$$F = \frac{\sum\limits_{i=1}^{k} n_i (\bar{y}_i - \bar{y})^2 / (k-1)}{\sum\limits_{i=1}^{k} \sum\limits_{j=1}^{n_i} (y_{ij} - \bar{y}_i)^2 / (N-k)}$$

Huber gave an F^* that is similar to F, but on which the outliers have less influence. In the numerator the first step is to replace $\bar{y}_i$ by $\hat{y}_i$. In a more general model Huber suggests to replace $\bar{y}$ by an ordinary least squares fit using $\hat{y}_i$ instead of y_i. In this case (without covariables) such a fit will yield the weighted mean:

$$\bar{y}_H = \frac{\sum\limits_{i=1}^{k} n_i \hat{y}_i}{N}$$

After scaling this modified numerator follows under mild conditions asymptotically a χ^2 distribution with the same number of degrees of freedom as the classical test.

Dealing with the denominator is a bit more difficult: one single outlier can be the cause of an extremely high value, so that H_0 can be accepted although the location parameters are very different. Huber proposes to replace the denominator by the folowing expression (where the influence of the outliers is reduced considerably):

$$\frac{1}{N-k} \frac{c^2 \sum\limits_{i=1}^{N} \Psi(\frac{r_i}{\hat{\sigma}})^2 \hat{\sigma}^2}{[\frac{1}{N} \sum\limits_{i=1}^{N} \Psi'(\frac{r_i}{\hat{\sigma}})]^2} \quad \text{where}$$

$$r_i = y_i - \hat{y}_i \quad \text{and}$$

$$c = 1 + \frac{k\,Var\,(\Psi')}{N\,[E(\Psi')]^2}.$$

$$\text{Here } E(\Psi') = \frac{1}{N} \sum\limits_{i=1}^{N} \Psi'(\frac{r_i}{\hat{\sigma}}) \text{ and}$$

$$Var\,(\Psi') = \frac{1}{N} \sum\limits_{i=1}^{N} [\Psi'(\frac{r_i}{\hat{\sigma}}) - E(\Psi')]^2.$$

These formulae are valid for every reasonable choice of Ψ. Since we use Huber's Ψ here they can be simplified considerably, because for Ψ' only the values 0 and 1 are possible. In this case we have:

$$c = 1 + k \frac{N-p}{Np}$$

Here p is the number of observations for which $\Psi'(\frac{r_i}{\hat{\sigma}}) = 1$. Just like in classical analysis of means H_0: $\mu_1 = \ldots = \mu_k$ is to be rejected if F^* exceeds the critical value of an F-distributed variate with k-1 and N-k degrees of freedom for some chosen size α. Huber claims that the approximation of F^* by an F-distribution is reasonable if all the samples contain at least five observations. This is the same condition that is usually put forward for using nonparametric tests with a χ^2-distribution.

It is fortunate that in analysis of means models the predictors are dummy-variables that do not contain any errors, because Huber's approach is very sensitive to situations where the predictors have outlying values. Covariables can be included in the model, provided that they do not contain outliers. The test can be generalized to more complex designs, including interactions. In this respect Huber's method seems more promising than its nonparametric alternatives, where the concept of rank-interaction is a complex matter, even in a simple two-way layout [De Kroon and Van der Laan (1981)].

5.6. The actual size of the tests

The probability of rejecting H_0 when true was estimated by using a simulation with 2000 replications. This was done for 3 and 6 groups, symmetric and one-sided contamination and sample sizes of 10, 25 and 40. The samples were generated from normal populations with $\mu_i = 0$ and $\sigma^2 = 1$. Symmetric contamination was simulated by using $\sigma^2 = 50$ with probabilities 0, 0.03 and 0.1. For trimming and winsorizing the constant g was chosen proportional to the sample sizes. The results of these simulations are presented in tables 1 and 2, where the estimated size for each simulation is given as the percentage of rejections for a test with nominal size $\alpha = 0.05$. Coded values for n_i and g are explained in table 3. In these tables the classical test is denoted as Anova.

In the case of one-sided contamination the use of $\sigma^2 = 50$ was restricted to positive observations. At the same time, the probability of a multiplication by 50 was doubled to 2ϵ, in order to get the same expected number of outliers as with symmetric contamination. The results of this simulation are presented in tables 4 and 5.

Table 1: Symmetric contamination, $k = 3$							
n_i	ϵ	g	Anova	VdW	Trim	Wins	Huber
10	0	2	4.95	4.15	5.25	5.25	5.45
10	0.03	2	3.95	4.10	5.00	5.20	5.15
10	0.1	2	2.85	4.90	5.70	5.45	5.25
25	0	3	4.80	5.05	5.40	5.05	5.35
25	0.03	3	3.25	4.20	4.80	4.75	5.20
25	0.1	3	4.00	5.05	4.95	6.40	5.40
40	0	5	5.15	4.95	5.15	4.65	5.00
40	0.03	5	5.15	5.20	5.30	4.80	5.25
40	0.1	5	4.35	4.65	4.70	5.45	4.60
A	0	B	4.45	3.80	3.90	3.85	4.40
A	0.03	B	4.85	5.00	4.10	4.40	5.70
A	0.1	B	5.30	4.75	4.25	4.95	5.25

Table 2: Symmetric contamination, $k = 6$							
n_i	ϵ	g	Anova	VdW	Trim	Wins	Huber
10	0	2	5.25	4.50	5.65	4.95	6.05
10	0.03	2	3.10	3.50	5.35	4.70	5.45
10	0.1	2	3.20	3.85	5.20	5.25	5.20
25	0	3	4.40	4.20	4.50	3.95	5.05
25	0.03	3	4.25	4.95	4.95	4.70	5.30
25	0.1	3	3.95	5.00	4.35	7.20	5.15
40	0	5	5.90	5.65	5.90	5.30	6.05
40	0.03	5	4.20	4.70	5.30	5.05	5.30
40	0.1	5	4.30	4.35	4.20	6.10	4.15
C	0	D	4.75	4.65	3.95	3.40	5.25
C	0.03	D	4.45	4.55	4.75	4.20	5.75
C	0.1	D	6.20	5.15	4.00	5.85	5.55

Table 3: The codes used	
Code	Meaning
A	10,25,40
B	2,3,5
C	10,10,25,25,40,40
D	2,2,3,3,5,5

Table 4: One-sided contamination, k = 3							
n_i	ϵ	g	Anova	VdW	Trim	Wins	Huber
10	0	2	4.75	4.15	5.60	5.45	6.35
10	0.03	2	4.00	4.75	5.75	5.70	5.65
10	0.1	2	3.75	5.00	5.20	5.35	5.65
25	0	3	5.65	5.20	5.30	5.20	6.00
25	0.03	3	3.80	4.40	4.75	4.65	5.20
25	0.1	3	3.50	4.90	3.90	7.50	5.15
40	0	5	4.85	4.70	4.60	4.10	4.60
40	0.03	5	4.75	5.25	5.45	5.15	5.80
40	0.1	5	4.95	5.60	4.75	9.40	5.55
A	0	B	5.10	5.35	4.60	4.50	5.65
A	0.03	B	4.35	4.80	4.40	4.50	5.30
A	0.1	B	4.90	4.55	3.60	6.05	5.35

The tables are not very clear if one wants to compare these tests. The standard deviation of the estimated size is $\sqrt{0.05*0.95/2000} = 0.00487$ or 0.487%. Let d be the percentage of rejected hypotheses minus 5 and divided by this standard deviation. Tables 6 and 7 show the values of d for each test. Three categories have been separated by double lines: $d < -2$ (conservative), $-2 \leqslant d < 2$ (accurate) and $2 \leqslant d$ (progressive). Tables 6 and 7 suggest the following conclusions:

- Classical analysis of means tends to be conservative in the presence of outliers.

Table 5: One-sided contamination, k = 6							
n_i	ϵ	g	Anova	VdW	Trim	Wins	Huber
10	0	2	5.80	4.65	4.85	5.10	6.10
10	0.03	2	3.95	4.60	5.90	5.75	6.15
10	0.1	2	3.15	5.05	4.85	5.20	6.35
25	0	3	4.55	4.15	5.00	4.55	5.20
25	0.03	3	5.55	5.20	5.35	6.00	5.90
25	0.1	3	4.15	4.90	4.25	11.80	5.65
40	0	5	4.15	4.35	4.30	3.55	4.30
40	0.03	5	4.40	4.90	4.55	4.90	4.95
40	0.1	5	4.35	4.10	3.55	12.70	4.10
C	0	D	5.55	4.95	4.60	4.55	6.20
C	0.03	D	5.20	4.80	3.95	4.30	5.55
C	0.1	D	5.90	5.15	4.05	9.15	6.15

Table 6: Symmetric contamination					
	Anova	VdW	Trim	Wins	Huber
$d < -3$	4	1		1	
$-3 \leqslant d < -2$	3	2	3	2	
$-2 \leqslant d < -1$	7	6	5	2	2
$-1 \leqslant d < 1$	8	14	13	15	17
$1 \leqslant d < 2$	1	1	3	1	3
$2 \leqslant d < 3$	1			2	2
$3 \leqslant d < 4$					
$4 \leqslant d < 5$				1	
$5 \leqslant d$					

- The method of Van der Waerden is unaffected concerning the size by this kind of non-normality, which is just what might be expected from a nonparametric test.

Table 7: One-sided contamination					
	Anova	VdW	Trim	Wins	Huber
$d <-3$	2				
$-3 \leqslant d <-2$	4		4	1	
$-2 \leqslant d <-1$	5	5	4	4	2
$-1 \leqslant d <1$	8	18	13	10	7
$1 \leqslant d <2$	5	1	3	2	8
$2 \leqslant d <3$				2	7
$3 \leqslant d <4$					
$4 \leqslant d <5$					
$5 \leqslant d$				5	

- The trimmed test seems slightly conservative in this situation, but less than classical analysis of means.

- Symmetric contamination does not seem to affect the Winsorized test very much, but this method is clearly not robust against one-sided contamination. Tables 4 and 5 show that the cases where $5 \leqslant d$ have a very high proportion of outliers: $\epsilon = 0.1$. Such values of ϵ make it possible that outliers are found in the body of a sample and not only in its tails (as defined by g). It would be unreasonable to expect robustness against this situation in a Winsorized test, because a tail consisting of outliers can enter the computation. This problem can not occur in a trimmed test.

- Huber's method seems the best for symmetric contamination, although the differences with the other tests are not convincing (only classical anova is too conservative). Against one-sided contamination the suggestion of a slight progressiveness exists. Values of d between 2 and 3 occurred in 7 cases. It is interesting to note that 4 of these cases contained no outliers ($\epsilon = 0$), so that the results for these rows in the tables for symmetric and one-sided contamination should be similar. An examination of all the results for Huber's method shows that indeed a very slight progressiveness exists, but that the contamination has almost no influence (see table 8).

Table 8: Huber's method	
Contamination	Estimated size in %
none ($\epsilon = 0$)	5.437
symmetric	5.228
one-sided	5.528

The estimated sizes in table 8 are based on 16*2000 replications, so that their standard deviation is $0.487/4 = 0.122$. Two of the three sizes differ significantly from 5% and it is clear that the approximation of Huber's test statistic by an F-distribution can be improved. But for practical purposes these results are acceptable.

5.7. A comparison of powers

Here a simulation study is presented that differs from the one in the previous section in only one respect: the samples were generated with unequal location parameters. Table 9 is based on symmmetric contamination with three samples. Tables were generated also from symmetric contamination with k = 6 and one-sided contamination with k = 3 and k = 6, but the results were very similar and therefore they will not be presented here. A summary of these results is given in table 10, where the powers for uncontaminated data ($\epsilon = 0$) are the means of 16 separate simulations with 2000 replications each. The other results are based on 8 simulations with the same number of replications. Table 10 suggests the following conclusions:

-   Classical analysis of means is the most powerful test for normal data, but contamination reduces the power of this method considerably. It does not matter whether the contamination is symmetric or one-sided; only the number of outliers (for some chosen variance) appears to have any influence.

Table 9: Symmetric contamination, k = 3								
n_i	ϵ	g	μ_i	Anova	VdW	Trim	Wins	Huber
10	0	2	P	88.05	85.50	77.85	78.05	84.50
10	0.03	2	P	64.55	75.95	74.05	73.95	80.75
10	0.1	2	P	36.75	59.20	64.70	65.05	69.25
25	0	3	Q	88.20	87.25	84.45	84.50	85.45
25	0.03	3	Q	59.50	80.90	80.95	81.25	82.45
25	0.1	3	Q	29.00	63.25	69.05	69.15	71.00
40	0	5	R	89.55	89.30	87.15	87.30	87.05
40	0.03	5	R	57.30	82.15	82.95	82.90	83.65
40	0.1	5	R	27.45	66.15	73.65	74.10	75.50
A	0	B	S	92.65	92.10	86.95	86.85	91.00
A	0.03	B	S	64.75	86.20	83.10	83.10	87.35
A	0.1	B	S	31.25	72.00	74.80	75.55	80.45

μ_i	$10\mu_i$
P	0,8,16
Q	0,5,10
R	0,4,8
S	0,8,13

Table 10: Comparison of powers						
Contamination	ϵ	Anova	VdW	Trim	Wins	Huber
none	0	90.50	89.44	85.25	85.41	88.19
symmetric	0.03	59.63	82.06	81.70	81.70	84.68
	0.1	28.55	65.54	71.43	72.54	75.12
one-sided	0.03	59.59	82.99	81.71	81.78	85.19
	0.1	29.20	68.71	65.48	68.88	75.08

Table 9, as well as the tables that were not included in this chapter, show that the difference in power for normal data ($\epsilon = 0$) between classical anova and the test of Van der Waerden almost disappears as the sample size increases from 10 to 40. Even for small samples (n_i = 10) the difference is only marginal. The influence of outliers on Van der Waerden's test is considerably smaller than on classical analysis of means, especialy as their number increases.

- Trimming and Winsorizing give similar results, except for one-sided contamination with $\epsilon = 0.1$, where Winsorizing seems to provide a more powerful test. But that is just the situation where winsorizing should not be trusted because outliers can occur between the tails of a sample (as defined by g) resulting in a probability of rejecting H_0 when true that considerably exceeds the chosen size α. Table 7 shows that trimming is insensitive to this problem, at least with our values of g. For smaller values of ϵ, the values of g could be lowered, which might result in a somewhat higher power.

- Huber's method yields the most powerful test, except when the data come from uncontaminated normal distributions in which case classical analysis of means has slightly more power.

The aim of the study presented in this chapter was to select a test for outlier-resistant one-way analysis of means that could be added to the local collection of statistical software at Eindhoven University of Technology. Considering the accuracy of the actual size, and the superior power of Huber's method, the conclusion was reached that this test was the appropriate choice. However, the differences with Van der Waerden's test and trimming are moderate, and Huber's greater power may be partly attributed to its slightly greater size. So Van der Waerden's test and trimming can be considered as reasonable alternatives.

5.8. An example with one outlier

Consider the heights of people, coming from three groups. Every sample contains ten observations and the data are given in meters with two decimals. The results are presented in table 11. All tests reject the hypothesis H_0 of equal means. The results are:

Classical analysis of means: F = 6.64 with 2 and 27 degrees of freedom. The critical value for these parameters is 3.39 ($\alpha = 0.05$). Therefore H_0 can be rejected.

Van der Waerden: The test statistic is 9.49 with 2 degrees of freedom. The critical value for a χ^2-distributed variate here is 5.99 resulting is the same conclusion.

Table 11: Heights of people		
Group 1	Group 2	Group 3
1.88	1.86	1.56
1.81	1.75	1.67
1.99	1.78	1.57
1.84	1.77	1.72
1.89	1.80	1.90
1.90	1.71	1.80
1.97	1.87	1.76
1.85	1.92	1.77
1.88	1.60	1.73
1.91	1.68	1.95

Trimmed analysis of means: F = 5.44 with 2 and 21 degrees of freedom. The loss of 6 degrees of freedom for the denominator comes from deleting one observation from both tails in each sample. The critical level here is 3.47 so that the difference of the means remains significant.

Winsorized analysis of means: F = 5.75 with 2 and 21 degrees of freedom. The conclusion remains the same.

Huber's method: F = 6.65 with 2 and 27 degrees of freedom. This result is almost equal to that of the classical method.

Now suppose that for the first observation in the first group the decimal point is forgotten. So the value 1.88 is replaced by 188. And here we have a very serious outlier. What will happen to the results?

Classical: F = 1.10 with 2 and 27 degrees of freedom. The difference of the means has been masked by the presence of the outlier.

Van der Waerden: The test statistic is 10.63 with 2 degrees of freedom so that H_0 will still be rejected.

Trimmed test: F = 6.21 with 2 and 21 degrees of freedom. The conclusion is not affected by the presence of an outlier.

Winsorized test: F = 6.46 with 2 and 21 degrees of freedom. The conclusion is the same.

Huber's method: F = 9.30 with 2 and 27 degrees of freedom.

In the last line, just like with the other robust methods, the difference of the means has become more significant. In this respect there is quite a difference with classical analysis of means where the power has been absorbed completely by the presence of one single outlier.

5.9. Least median of squares

In this section and the following methods for outlier-resistant one-way analysis of means will be described that entered this study, but were discarded before the final simulation. The first method is Least Median of Squares (LMS) that originates from Rousseeuw (1984) and is designed for regression models. Instead of minimizing the sum of squares, LMS minimizes the median of the squared residuals. This results in very robust estimates for the parameters β_i: up to 50% outliers have no influence on the estimated values. No simple formula for this method seems to exist, but Leroy and Rousseeuw (1985) [or Rousseeuw and Leroy (1987)] present an heuristic algorithm that is easy to implement. LMS results in fitted values $\hat{y}_i^+$ that can be used to estimate the scale parameter:

$$\hat{\sigma}^+ = 1.4826 \sqrt{med_i (y_i - \hat{y}_i^+)^2}(1 + 5/(N-k))$$

Here N is the number of observations for a regression model with k parameters. The next step is to delete observations y_i if:

$$\frac{|y_i - \hat{y}_i^+|}{\hat{\sigma}^+} > 2.5$$

If the residuals are normally distributed, roughly 2% of the observations will be deleted. The remaining observations are thereafter used in an ordinary regression, where tests of significance can be performed as if these observations were the only ones in the analysis. In regression situations the results of this approach are very satisfactory, and therefore it seemed attractive to try LMS for anova models. The LMS estimate of location is the midpoint of the shortest half of the ordered observations. This was used to estimate the parameters in the one-way analysis of means model in this study. Thereafter the outliers were deleted and a classical test was performed on the remaining observations. Since LMS was only validated for continuous predictors it was necessary to verify the control over the chosen size again, because here it was used with dummy variables. The results of a simulation were rather disappointing: with a nominal size of 5% the estimated size varied between 9% and 26% in similar tables as where the size was estimated for the other tests. The results were especially bad when there were no outliers ($\epsilon = 0$), or if the samples were small. This can be explained as follows. The LMS estimate of location is very robust, but not very efficient. If a sample happens to be seriously skewed one can expect that σ will be under-estimated. This results in deleting more observations than the probability of $|u| > 2.5$ indicates (where u denotes a standard normal distributed variate). Since the deleted observations are the ones that differ most from the estimate of location, this will lead to under-estimating the within-variance, while leaving the between-variance relatively unaffected. This explains the fact that the values of F exceed their expectations under H_0. In the presence of outliers the deleted observations will be the ones that ought to be deleted. And for bigger samples the probability of being seriously skewed decreases.

So LMS is in its present stage not a good candidate for outliers-resistant analysis of means. We need more insight in the distribution of the test-statistic under H_0, since the way the F-statistic is used here is certainly not appropriate. There is however a situation with a nominal predictor where LMS could be considered. Suppose there are some continuous covariables. Then LMS can be used for every value of the nominal predictor. The outliers can be deleted and ordinary regression can be applied to the remaining observations. Of course this can only be done if the nominal predictor has only a few different values, and many observations for each value. An attractive property of LMS, that might prove useful here, is its insensitivity to leverage points (points with outlying values for the predictor variables). In that respect LMS is far better than Huber's method that can also handle covariables but only in the absence of leverage points.

5.10. An adaptive nonparametric test

For a short while it seemed possible to construct an adaptive non-parametric test with reasonable power for the contamination models used in this study. The approach was strongly related to the distributions under consideration. The density for symmetric contamination is:

$$f(x) = \epsilon \frac{1}{\sigma \sqrt{\theta 2\pi}} \exp[-\frac{x^2}{2\theta\sigma^2}] + (1-\epsilon) \frac{1}{\sigma \sqrt{2\pi}} \exp[-\frac{x^2}{2\sigma^2}]$$

Suppose we are sure that this model represents the data, and that we know the parameters ϵ, σ and θ. For this distribution it is possible to construct a nonparametric test with asymptotically optimal power. The test-statistic is given by:

$$Q = \frac{N-1}{\sum\limits_{i=1}^{N} (a_i - \bar{a})^2} \sum\limits_{j=1}^{k} \frac{[S_j - E(S_j)]^2}{n_j}$$

This denotes a large family of which the Mood & Brown, Kruskal & Wallis and Van der Waerden tests are members. The scores a_i can be chosen in order to get optimal power for some selected distribution. S_j is the sum of the scores within the j-th sample. The statistic Q is asymptotically distributed as χ^2 with k - 1 degrees of freedom [Hajek (1969)] if the score-generating function ϕ is reasonably smooth. The scores are generated as:

$$a_i = \phi(\frac{i}{N+1}, f)$$

In order to get asymptotically optimal power for some distribution F with density f the function ϕ has to be chosen as follows:

$$\phi(u, f) = -\frac{f'[F^{-1}(u)]}{f[F^{-1}(u)]}$$

Using these principles it is possible to construct an optimal test for the distribution that represents symmetric contamination. And if the parameters are not known they can be estimated. The estimated values can then be used in the density function and this would result in a nonparametric test with satisfactory power for the contamination model if the parameters were efficiently estimated. The first parameter to be estimated is σ. This can be done by using a robust regression procedure like Huber's or LMS. Fitting the model will result in $\hat{\sigma}$ and fitted values $\hat{y}_i$ for the observations y_i. The residuals are given as $e_i = y_i - \hat{y}_i$. And with these it is possible to estimate the other parameters ϵ and θ. Suppose x is a normally distributed stochastic variable with zero mean and variance σ^2. Then we have $E|x| = \sigma\sqrt{2/\pi}$ and $Ex^2 = \sigma^2$. These moments can be estimated as $\frac{1}{N}\sum\limits_{i=1}^{N}|e_i|$ and $\frac{1}{N}\sum\limits_{i=1}^{N}e_i^2$ respectively. Combining this with the known density of the errors results in the following two equations:

$$\frac{1}{N}\sum_{i=1}^{N}|e_i| = (1-\epsilon)\sigma\sqrt{2/\pi} + \epsilon\sigma\sqrt{2\theta/\pi}$$

$$\frac{1}{N}\sum_{i=1}^{N}e_i^2 = (1-\epsilon)\sigma^2 + \epsilon\theta\sigma^2$$

After substituting the robust estimate $\hat{\sigma}$ for σ the parameters ϵ and θ can be estimated from these equations.

Some experiments have led to the conclusion that the sample size needed for a reasonable estimate of the parameters σ, ϵ and θ by far exceeds the sample sizes that are common for analysis of means situations. And this is not the only reason for rejecting this approach. A test like this will be strongly adapted to the chosen model for the outliers. And even if this test would show good power in a simulation where the distribution of the errors matches the model on which the computation of the scores is based, almost nothing could be said about its behaviour for other models describing the outliers.

5.11. Robustness of Huber's method against variance heterogeneity

Since Huber's method was selected as the best choice for normal populations with some extreme outliers it is interesting to examine what will happen if this test is used in situations where the second order method of James [see chapter 2] is recommended. If we examine the different scale parameters relative to the smallest one, it is possible to describe the situation of variance heterogeneity in the language of this chapter. The parameter θ is not the same for every group, but the values for θ_i are moderate. For every group the parameter $\epsilon_i = 1$ except for the group with the smallest variance where $\epsilon_i = 0$. So variance heterogeneity is quite different from the model with outliers.

Every entry in table 12 is based on 2500 replications, so that the actual size is estimated with a standard deviation of 0.436% for a nominal size of 5%. The conclusion is very clear: Huber's method is not robust against variance heterogeneity. The behaviour of this test is similar to that of classical anova [see chapter 1]. If the sample sizes are equal and the population variances are unequal then the actual probability of rejecting a hypothesis when true will exceed the nominal value. If the sample sizes are unequal then the test will become even more progressive if the bigger variances coincide with the smaller samples. Conservatism can be expected if the bigger variances coincide with the bigger samples.

Table 12: Huber's method		
sample size	sigma	percentage
10,10,10	1,1,1	6.16
	1,2,3	10.08
25,25,25	1,1,1	5.16
	1,2,3	12.16
40,40,40	1,1,1	5.96
	1,2,3	12.36
10,25,40	1,1,1	5.28
	1,2,3	2.16
	3,2,1	24.60
10,10,10,10,10,10	1,1,1,1,1,1	5.12
	1,1,2,2,3,3	12.28
25,25,25,25,25,25	1,1,1,1,1,1	5.40
	1,1,2,2,3,3	16.36
40,40,40,40,40,40	1,1,1,1,1,1	4.80
	1,1,2,2,3,3	15.32
10,10,25,25,40,40	1,1,1,1,1,1	5.84
	1,1,2,2,3,3	3.48
	3,3,2,2,1,1	25.16

What is the practical value of a test that is outlier-resistant but not robust against variance heterogeneity? It can handle some typing errors if the data are entered at a computer-terminal. It can also handle some really extreme observations as long as they are evenly distributed over the samples. But Huber's method can certainly not be recommended if there are reasons to suppose that the scale parameters of the populations involved are different.

5.12. Robustness of the second order method of James against outliers

In chapter 2 we saw that the second order method of James gives the user excellent control over the chosen size and has reasonable power in most situations. The only condition is that the samples come from normal populations. Variance homogeneity is not assumed. In this section the behaviour of the method of James will be examined in the presence of outliers. Table 13 presents a simulation study under the hypothesis

Table 13: James method (size)		
sample size	ϵ	percentage
10,10,10	0	4.80
	0.03	3.15
	0.1	1.85
25,25,25	0	4.75
	0.03	4.00
	0.1	2.30
40,40,40	0	5.10
	0.03	3.25
	0.1	3.80
10,25,40	0	5.10
	0.03	3.70
	0.1	2.90
10,10,10,10,10,10	0	5.50
	0.03	3.85
	0.1	2.00
25,25,25,25,25,25	0	5.10
	0.03	3.65
	0.1	2.50
40,40,40,40,40,40	0	5.25
	0.03	2.70
	0.1	2.95
10,10,25,25,40,40	0	5.00
	0.03	3.95
	0.1	2.40

H_0 that the location parameters are equal. From table 13 we can conclude that an error distribution with outliers can make the method of James conservative. This simulation was based on 2000 replications for each cell. The samples were generated from normal populations with μ_i = 0 and σ^2 = 1. With probability ϵ the variance was increased to σ^2 = 50.

Conservatism in a test usually results in a loss of power. To get a first impression the method of James was applied to the data representing the heights of people from three groups that was mentioned earlier in this chapter. This resulted in a tail probability of 0.002, so that the

Table 14: James method (power)					
sample size	ϵ	$10\mu_i$	Anova	James	Huber
10,10,10	0	0,8,16	88.05	84.70	84.50
	0.03		64.55	69.85	80.75
	0.1		36.75	43.20	69.25
25,25,25	0	0,5,10	88.20	87.30	85.45
	0.03		59.50	66.20	82.45
	0.1		29.00	33.90	71.00
40,40,40	0	0,4,8	89.55	88.60	87.05
	0.03		57.30	62.55	83.65
	0.1		27.45	30.90	75.50
10,25,40	0	0,8,13	92.65	89.75	91.00
	0.03		64.75	71.30	87.35
	0.1		31.25	44.30	80.45

hypothesis of equal means could be rejected without any doubt. Then the decimal point of the first observation in the first group was removed. Instead of 1.88 we got 188 and this resulted in a tail probability of 0.525. So one outlier can remove all power from this test, just like we already saw for classical one-way analysis of means.

Table 14 presents a comparison of the powers of James test with classical analysis of means and Huber's method. If there are no outliers ($\epsilon = 0$) the difference in power is very small. The classical method is the best, and James test seems slightly better than Huber's method, but more simulations should be done before the difference would be convincing. If the fraction of outliers increases to 0.03 and 0.1, then the power of James test decreases, but not so fast as the power of the classical method. Compared with these two, Huber's method is very outlier-resistant.

The conclusion can be that the method of James is not to be recommended if there are reasons to suppose that outliers may be present. In practice it will not always be easy to determine whether a more robust method than classical anova is needed. And it is very unfortunate that the methods of James and Huber, that have excellent characteristics in the situations for which they are designed, are not robust against variance heterogeneity as well as outliers. So the user of these methods has the difficult task to choose carefully.

In the introduction we saw already some kind of preliminary data analysis that involves the extreme values of every sample, as well as the quartiles. Q_2 is the median and that is a more robust estimate of location than the sample mean. The difference between Q_1 and Q_3 is an indication of the scale and the values for these differences should be similar if one is considering a test that assumes variance homogeneity. The classical variances or standard deviations are not suitable for this purpose if one is taking the possible presence of some extreme outliers into account. A more robust alternative is based on the MAD estimate of scale:

$$S_{MAD} = 1.4826 med_i |x_i - med_j (x_j)|$$

Here MAD stands for Median of the Absolute Deviations from the median. A more attractive kind of preliminary data analysis than the one given in section 1.4 is given in table 15:

Table 15: Preliminary data description				
sample	minimum	median	S_{MAD}	maximum
1	1.56	1.73	0.124	1.87
2	1.58	1.75	0.151	1.90
3	1.61	1.79	0.148	1.88
4	1.57	1.80	0.160	185

The data represent the heights of people, coming from 4 groups. It is easily seen that variance homogeneity can be assumed here (if the sample sizes are moderate), but that the analyst has made a typing error. In this case it is more appropriate to replace the observation 185 by 1.85 and try a similar data description again in order to find out if there are more typing errors of this kind. But in other situations one might prefer an outlier-resistant method.

6. Robustness of multiple comparisons against variance heterogeneity and outliers

6.1. Introduction

In the preceding chapters we saw that the second order James test is very robust against variance heterogeneity and that Huber's method can handle some extreme outliers. Both tests are designed for the hypothesis of equal population parameters, and acceptance of this hypothesis is usually the end of the analysis. But if the location parameters seem to be unequal a new question arises and that concerns some kind of grouping of the samples. For the moment we will consider samples from normal populations with equal variances and no outliers. Fisher (1935) suggested the Least Significant Difference test that consists of two stages. At first an ordinary one-way analysis of means is performed and if the hypothesis is accepted then no further action is taken. But if the hypothesis is rejected than all the pairs are compared with a Students t-test with the same size α. The standard error is based on the pooled variance from all the samples with the appropriate number of degrees of freedom. The t-tests are preceded by the F-test as some kind of protection against loss of control over the chosen size. Suppose the analysis consisted of only the paired t-tests with the same size $\alpha = 0.05$. Then the probability of declairing any pair different when in fact their location parameters are equal can easily exceed this chosen size. Duncan (1951) showed that the actual size in this context will be about 0.1223 for 3 samples, 0.2034 for 4 samples and even 0.9183 for 20 samples. So some kind of protection is needed and Fisher's idea works if one only wants to protect the overall size if all the location parameters are equal. But suppose there are some groups of samples having different means, but that within these groups the samples come from populations with the same means. For instance, we can have 10 samples, 5 of them with expectation μ_1 and 5 with expectation μ_2. Then the F-test will not give the necessary protection, because after rejection of the overall hypothesis the t-tests will be applied to every pair with the same α. Hayter (1986) has examined this situation and he proved the following theorem:

> For any balanced one-way model and for an unbalanced model with k = 3 the Maximum Familywise Error Rate MFWER of the α level Least Significant Difference test of k populations with ν degrees of freedom for the error is:

$$\alpha^*(k,\nu,\alpha) = P[q_{k-1,\nu} > \sqrt{2}\,t_\nu(\alpha/2)]$$

> Here $q_{k-1,\nu}$ is a studentized range random variable with parameters k-1 and ν, and $t_\nu(\alpha/2)$ is the upper $\alpha/2$ point of the t-distribution with ν degrees of freedom.

The M in MFWER denotes that the maximum is taken over all possible values of the population means μ_i. Hayter also showed that $\alpha^*(k,\nu,\alpha)$ provides an upper bound on the MFWER for any unbalanced one-way model with more than three samples. Therefore the Least Significant Difference test can be improved by using $q_{k-1,\nu}(\alpha)/\sqrt{2}$ instead of $t_\nu(\alpha/2)$ for the pairwise comparisons in the second stage of this test. Adaptations of this idea to variance heterogeneity and to outliers will be discussed further in this chapter. First attention will be given to simple pairwise comparisons that are not protected by an overall test, but by modifications of the pairwise size α.

6.2. Pairwise comparisons based on the t-distribution

In this section we will drop the equality of the population variances. The pairwise comparisons need a procedure for the Behrens-Fisher problem and a good candidate is Welch's approximate t-solution. This test has been evaluated by Wang (1971) and he concluded that it gives the user excellent control over the chosen size, whatever the value of the nuisance parameter $\theta = \sigma_i^2/\sigma_j^2$ may be. The test statistic is:

$$t = \frac{x_i - x_j}{\sqrt{s_i^2/n_i + s_j^2/n_j}}$$

Here x_i denotes the i-th sample mean, s_i^2 the corresponding sample variance and n_i the sample size. Pooling of the k variances as in the second stage of Fishers Least Significant Difference test is avoided here.

The test statistic t follows under the hypothesis of equal population means approximately a t-distribution with ν_{ij} degrees of freedom:

$$\nu_{ij} = \frac{(\frac{s_i^2}{n_i} + \frac{s_j^2}{n_j})^2}{\frac{s_i^4}{n_i^2(n_i-1)} + \frac{s_j^4}{n_j^2(n_j-1)}}$$

Ury and Wiggings (1971) proposed this test for pairwise comparisons with the Bonferroni β that controls the familywise error rate if these comparisons are not preceeded by an overall test. For k samples there are $k(k-1)/2$ pairs. Therefore the probability of declaring any pair different when in fact they are equal is limited by α if for β the following value is chosen:

$$\beta = \frac{2\alpha}{k(k-1)}$$

The result will be conservative if one considers the familywise error rate. Another problem seems to lie in the fact that ν_{ij} is generally not an integer. But Wang has shown that replacing it by the nearest integer is a reasonable solution provided that ν_{ij} is not too small. An alternative is to use Peiser's (1943) approximation for which the parameter does not need to be an integer:

$$t_\nu(\alpha) \approx u_\alpha + \frac{1}{4\nu}[u_\alpha^3 + u_\alpha]$$

Here u_α stands for the upper α point of the standard normal distribution. The simultaneous confidence intervals for the Ury and Wiggins test are given by:

$$\mu_i - \mu_j \in [x_i - x_j \mp t_{\nu_{ij}}(\beta/2)\sqrt{s_i^2/n_i + s_j^2/n_j}]$$

There are some alternatives mentioned in the literature. Hochberg (1976) suggested using.

$$\mu_i - \mu_j \in [x_i - x_j \mp \gamma_\alpha \sqrt{s_i^2/n_i + s_j^2/n_j}]$$

Here γ_α is the solution of:

$$\sum_{i=1}^{k} \sum_{j=i+1}^{k} P[|t_{\nu_{ij}}| > \gamma] = \alpha$$

Here the same ν_{ij} is used as in the previous test. Tamhane (1979) has shown that these tests are very similar in all respects (if all the sample sizes are equal, the tests are even exactly the same). And since the Ury and Wiggins approach is easier to apply no further attention will be given to Hochberg's proposal. Tamhane (1977) suggested using Banerjee's (1961) approximate solution of the Behrens-Fisher problem with Sidak's γ for the pairwise comparisons. This γ also results in a conservative overall test, but it exceeds the Bonferroni β and therefore reduces the conservatism:

$$\gamma = 1 - (1-\alpha)^{\frac{2}{k(k-1)}}$$

This approach results in the following confidence intervals:

$$\mu_i - \mu_j \in [x_i - x_j \mp \sqrt{t_{\nu_i}^2 (\gamma/2)s_i^2/n_i + t_{\nu_j}^2 (\gamma/2)s_j^2/n_j}]$$

Later Tamhane (1979) showed that this will result in a very conservative test and he suggested to use the Welch test with γ instead of β for the pairwise comparisons. Ury and Wiggins (1971) found that the choice of ν_{ij} can be improved by taking $n_i + n_j - 2$ if one of the following conditions is met:

$$9/10 \leqslant n_i/n_j \leqslant 10/9$$

$$9/10 \leqslant (s_i^2/n_i)/(s_j^2/n_j) \leqslant 10/9$$

$$4/5 \leqslant n_i/n_j \leqslant 5/4 \text{ and } 1/2 \leqslant (s_i^2/n_i)/(s_j^2/n_j) \leqslant 2$$

$$2/3 \leqslant n_i/n_j \leqslant 3/2 \text{ and } 3/4 \leqslant (s_i^2/n_i)/(s_j^2/n_j) \leqslant 4/3$$

Tamhane (1979) showed that among some competitors this is the best test for pairwise comparisons based on the t-distribution. Further in this chapter some alternatives will be discussed that use other distributions. For equal variances the natural choice is:

$$\mu_i - \mu_j \in [x_i - x_j \mp t_\nu(\gamma/2)s \sqrt{1/n_i + 1/n_j}]$$

Here the standard deviation s is based on the pooled variance with $\nu = N - k$ degrees of freedom. An adaptation of this method to the situation of equal variances with a small probability of some extreme outliers will also be discussed (see section 7 of this chapter).

6.3. Multiple range tests

In this section a strategy will be pointed out that was originated by Newman (1939), Duncan (1951) and Keuls (1952). At first we will assume the sample sizes to be equal. Also variance heterogeneity will not be allowed. Later on these restrictions will be dropped.

Let $x_{(1)}, \ldots, x_{(k)}$ be the sample means, sorted in non-decreasing order. The first hypothesis of interest is $H_0: \mu_1 = \ldots = \mu_k$, where the population means are renumbered so that their ordering becomes the same as the sample means which are their estimates. Then H_0 can be tested with:

$$\mu_1 - \mu_k \in [x_1 - x_k \mp q_{k,\nu}(\alpha) \frac{s}{\sqrt{n}}]$$

Here $q_{k,\nu}(\alpha)$ is the upper α point of the studentized range distribution with parameters k and ν. The standard deviation s is based on the pooled variance with $\nu = N - k$ degrees of freedom:

$$s^2 = \frac{1}{\nu} \sum_{i=1}^{k} \sum_{j=1}^{n} (x_{ij} - x_i)^2$$

Duncan (1951) remarks that this test has a serious disadvantage relative to the F-test for one-way analysis of means:

> When an F-test is used the null hypothesis has a smaller likelihood in every case in which it is rejected than in every case in which it is accepted. This is not true for a range test. For that test, the null hypothesis is sometimes rejected in cases when it has a larger likelihood than in other cases when it is accepted. This is a decided intuitive weakness of any test of a null hypothesis which does not conform to the likelihood ratio

criterion.

If H_0 is rejected, the next stage is to test $\mu_1 = \ldots = \mu_{k-1}$ and $\mu_2 = \ldots = \mu_k$. Proceeding like this until every hypothesis is accepted will result in some kind of grouping of the samples such that μ_i and μ_j will be called significantly different if they do not belong to the same group. It is possible that the resulting groups partially overlap, so that the following situation can be met:

$\mu_1 = \mu_2$: accepted

$\mu_2 = \mu_3$: accepted

$\mu_1 = \mu_3$: rejected

This is only natural; pairwise comparisons often will yield similar results. If a candidate for the splitting process contains p means then $q_{p,\nu}(\alpha_p)$ is to be used instead of $q_{k,\nu}(\alpha)$. Newman and Keuls suggested $\alpha_p = \alpha$ and Duncan preferred:

$$\alpha_p^D = 1 - (1-\alpha)^{p-1}$$

The Newman and Keuls α_p will only guarantee the overall size α for the hypothesis that all the means are equal. Duncan's method does not control the familywise error rate, but it controls each pairwise comparison at the α level. Both choices will be discarded since in this chapter we are more interested in controlling the MFWER. This can be done by following a suggestion of Ryan (1960) for which Einot and Gabriel (1975) demonstrated that the actual probability of declaring any mean different when in fact they are equal will never exceed α:

$$\alpha_p^R = 1 - (1-\alpha)^{p/k}$$

Now the equality of the sample sizes will be dropped, but for the moment the variances still have to be equal. Miller (1966) suggested using the median of $n_1, \ldots, n_k$. Winer (1962) suggested the harmonic mean H:

$$H = \frac{1}{\frac{1}{k}\sum_{i=1}^{k}\frac{1}{n_i}}$$

Kramer (1956) modified the formula of the test to this situation:

$$\mu_i - \mu_j \in [x_i - x_j \mp q_{p,\nu}(\alpha_p)s\sqrt{(1/n_i + 1/n_j)/2}]$$

Here $\nu = N - k$ and $N = \sum_{i=1}^{k} n_i$. Only in Kramer's case (and then only for two samples) does the studentized range distribution hold. For Miller and Winer the approximation will be reasonable if the sample sizes are not too different. Kramer's test contains a trap that can be explained by considering four samples with unequal sample sizes. Let $x_{(1)}, \dots, x_{(4)}$ be the ordered sample means and $n_1, \dots, n_4$ the corresponding sample sizes. Suppose that n_1 and n_4 are much smaller than n_2 and n_3. Then the hypothesis $\mu_1 = \dots = \mu_4$ can be accepted while μ_2 and μ_3 are significantly different. But the strategy will make sure that this difference will never be found. This problem was pointed out by a referee of Kramer's contribution and it was mentioned in the revised publication.

From here on the variances will be allowed to be unequal. For equal sample sizes Ramseyer and Tcheng (1973) found that the studentized range statistic is remarkably robust against variance heterogeneity. So for almost equal sample sizes it seems reasonable to use the Winer or Miller approach and ignore the differences in the variances. But suppose that in the above mentioned example the variances s_2^2 and s_3^2 are much smaller than s_1^2 and s_4^2 (this is a situation that was not considered by Ramseyer and Tcheng). Then it is possible that a pairwise comparison of μ_2 and μ_3 would lead to a significant result, while the hypothesis for some group of samples to which these means belong is accepted. So the pairwise comparison will never be performed and here we have a conflict between the stepwise strategy and the individual tests.

Unfortunately, the robustness of Kramer's test is rather poor [Games and Howell (1976)], so if the sample sizes differ greatly one might be tempted to consider:

$$\mu_i - \mu_j \in [x_i - x_j \mp q_{p,\nu_{ij}}(\alpha_p) \sqrt{(s_i^2/n_i + s_j^2/n_j)/2}]$$

Here pooling of the variances is avoided and ν_{ij} comes from Welch's test and is restricted to the extreme samples in the range under consideration. The studentized range distribution does not hold for these separately estimated variances, but in another context the approximation seems reasonable though a bit conservative as we will see in the next section. However the conflict with the strategy of the multiple range test is even stronger here, because if the extreme samples have big variances or small sample sizes it is possible that important differences within the range are obscured.

The conclusion from this section can be that generalisations of the multiple range test to unequal sample sizes or variance heterogeneity are not to be recommended. An important difference between two means can be masked by the presence of some small samples or some samples with bigger variances. Within the strategy of pairwise comparisons however, the studentized range distribution is a very attractive tool for unbalanced designs with variance heterogeneity as will be shown in the next section.

6.4. Pairwise comparisons based on the q-distribution

If the sample sizes and the variances are equal one can use Tukey's (1953) method for pairwise comparisons:

$$\mu_i - \mu_j \in [x_i - x_j \mp q_{k,\nu}(\alpha) \frac{s}{\sqrt{n}}]$$

Here s is based on the pooled variance with $\nu = N - k$ degrees of freedom. This test is known as the Tukey Wholly Significant Difference test and Miller (1966) has stated that it is the most powerful test for pairwise comparisons that controls the familywise error rate. An important difference of this test with Hayter's modification of Fisher's Least Significant Difference test that was mentioned in the introduction lies in the fact that Tukey uses $q_{k,\nu}(\alpha)$ while Hayter suggested

$q_{k-1,\nu}(\alpha)$. This difference comes from the fact that Tukey considers unprotected pairwise comparisons while in Hayter's case the pairwise comparisons are only performed if the hypothesis that all the means are equal is rejected by an α level F-test.

If the sample sizes are unequal one can consider Kramer's modification:

$$\mu_i - \mu_j \in [x_i - x_j \mp q_{k,\nu}(\alpha)s \sqrt{(1/n_i + 1/n_j)/2}]$$

Games and Howell (1976) mention that this puts the familywise error rate slightly below α, while using the median or the harmonic mean often results in exceeding α. They based the conservatism of the Tukey-Kramer method on a simulation study. Later (1984) Hayter gave an analytical proof for this conjecture. Games and Howell recommended Kramer's idea and suggested the following modification for unequal variances:

$$\mu_i - \mu_j \in [x_i - x_j \mp q_{k,\nu_{ij}}(\alpha)\sqrt{(s_i^2/n_i + s_j^2/n_j)/2}]$$

Here ν_{ij} comes from Welch's modified t-test. Therefore this method differs from pairwise comparisons based on Welch's test with Sidak's γ only in the factor that scales the combined standard deviation. Tamhane (1979) has shown that:

$$q_{k,\nu_{ij}}(\alpha)/\sqrt{2} \leqslant t_{\nu_{ij}}(\gamma/2) \text{ with } \gamma = 1-(1-\alpha)^{\frac{2}{k(k-1)}}$$

Here the equality only holds if k = 2. Therefore the test by Games and Howell will be more powerful. But they use the studentized range statistic in combination with separately estimated variances so there is some reason to fear that the actual familywise error rate will exceed its nominal value. In 1983 Games and Howell mentioned that for their test this error rate varied between 0.0286 and 0.0622 for a nominal value of 0.05 in a study with a wide variety of conditions.

In chapter 2 we saw that the second order method of James is a good choice for the hypothesis that all the means are equal. This test can handle variance heterogeneity very well, but it is not designed for multiple comparisons and therefore the Games and Howell test seems more attractive for cases where more information about the separate means is needed. In a simulation study both tests are compared under $H_0: \mu_1 = \ldots = \mu_k$ as well as under some alternatives. For the Games and Howell test the hypothesis H_0 is considered to be rejected if at least one pairwise comparison leads to a significant result. Each entry in tables 1 and 2 is based on 2500 replications.

Table 1: Actual size with nominal size = 5%			
sample size	σ_i	G&H	James
4,4,4,4	1,1,1,1	4.52	4.64
	1,2,2,3	6.08	5.84
4,6,8,10	1,1,1,1	3.20	4.56
	1,2,2,3	2.60	4.72
	3,2,2,1	4.88	5.64
10,10,10,10	1,1,1,1	2.44	5.36
	1,2,2,3	3.20	5.52
4,6,8,10,12	1,2,3,4,5	3.84	4.68
	1,2,3,5,7	3.84	4.92
	5,4,3,2,1	6.72	5.72
	7,5,3,2,1	6.64	5.92
8,8,8,8,8	1,2,3,4,5	4.60	4.56
	1,2,3,5,7	4.20	4.68

From table 1 it is clear that the test by James controls the chosen size much better than the Games and Howell method, which can be conservative but also slightly progressive. The pattern is similar as in classical one-way analysis of means: If the bigger samples coincide with the bigger variances then the Games and Howell test will be conservative. For more balanced situations the conservatism will decrease but not vanish. And if the bigger samples coincide with the smaller variances then the test will become slightly progressive if the differences are not too small.

A comparison of powers is given in table 2. It is remarkable that although the method of James has more power, the difference with the

Games and Howell test is only moderate, even in cases where the actual size of this test was reduced to 2.60% while a nominal value of 5% was chosen.

Table 2: Estimated power with nominal size = 5%				
sample size	μ_i	σ_i	G&H	James
4,4,4,4	3,0,0,0	1,1,1,1	86.00	86.84
		1,2,2,3	52.76	60.28
		3,2,2,1	21.56	22.72
	5,0,0,$\frac{1}{2}$	1,1,1,1	99.68	99.64
		1,2,2,3	91.60	97.08
		3,2,2,1	43.16	43.72
4,6,8,10	3,0,0,0	1,1,1,1	88.24	92.88
		1,2,2,3	75.60	86.92
		3,2,2,1	20.12	24.12
	0,0,0,3	1,2,2,3	47.80	50.40
		3,2,2,1	87.12	94.64

The conclusion of these simulations can be that for the hypothesis that all the means are equal the method of James is a better choice than the Games and Howell test. If one is interested in an adaptation of Fisher's Least Significant Difference test to the situation of variance hetero-geneity, a good start will be to replace the first-stage F-test by the method of James. Considering the results of this chapter and Hayter's suggestion a good candidate for the second stage of this test is:

$$\mu_i - \mu_j \in [x_i - x_j \mp q_{k-1,\nu_{ij}}(\alpha)\sqrt{(s_i^2/n_i + s_j^2/n_j)/2}]$$

The difference with the unprotected Games and Howell approach lies in the fact that here $q_{k-1,\nu_{ij}}(\alpha)$ is used instead of $q_{k,\nu_{ij}}(\alpha)$. Whichever approach the user may prefer, in both cases the q statistic is a very good tool for this kind of simultaneous statistical inference. Similar methods for a model with outliers will be given further in this chapter (see sectons 7, 8 and 9).

6.5. Multiple F-tests

This test was proposed by Duncan (1951). In the original version the population variances must be equal. The procedure is the same as for the multiple range test, only the q-statistic is replaced by an F, so that the first stage becomes classical one-way analysis of means. In every stage the pooled variance is used with the appropriate number of degrees of freedom, based on all the samples and not only on the ones within the range under consideration. At first Duncan proposed using $\alpha_p^D = 1-(1-\alpha)^{p-1}$ in order to set the error rate for pairwise comparisons to α. The operating characteristics of this approach are similar to repeated t-tests at level α if the sample sizes are not too different [Petrinovich and Hardyck (1969)]. Later (1955) Duncan suggested what he called protection levels for which the familywise error rate will never exceed α if the sample sizes are equal:

$$\alpha_p^{D^*} = 1-(1-\alpha)^{(p-1)/(k-1)}$$

This $\alpha_p^{D^*}$ will always be lower than Ryan's $\alpha_p^R = 1-(1-\alpha)^{p/k}$ except in the first stage when the value for both will be the chosen size α. And since α_p^R already controls the familywise error rate, Duncan's suggestion will not be considered further. Welsch (1977) found that even α_p^R can be improved a little and he suggested:

$$\alpha_p^W = 1-(1-\alpha)^{p/k} \text{ for } p < k-1$$

$$\alpha_p^W = \alpha \text{ for } p \geqslant k-1$$

In the context of the strategy with ordered sample means $\alpha_p^{D^*}$, α_p^R and α_p^W are only safe to control the familywise error rate if the design is balanced. The strategy can be adapted to the situation of unbalanced designs as we will see further in this section. For the moment we will simply ignore this and examine what can happen. The nature of the F-test allows unequal sample sizes. This seems to make this approach more attractive than the multiple range test, but there is a problem. Consider four samples with only a few observations for the smallest and largest sample mean and considerable sample sizes for the second and third ordered mean. If $H_0: \mu_1 = \ldots = \mu_4$ is rejected, the next two hypoheses to be tested are $\mu_1 = ... = \mu_3$ and $\mu_2 = ... = \mu_4$. So μ_1 and μ_4 will always be called different. But in this unbalanced design it is possible that a pairwise comparison of μ_1 and μ_4 would not yield any significance. One can of course apply an α level t-test to every pair that seems significant as a result of the multiple F-test. But it will not be easy to predict the effect of this approach on the familywise error rate.

Now the equality of the variances will be dropped. It is well known that the F-test is not robust against variance heterogeneity [Brown and Forsythe (1974), Ekbohm (1976)]. So it seems reasonable to use the non-iterative version of the second order method of James [see chapter 2], thus making a Multiple James test. This new test contains the same problem as the multiple F-test, but that is not all. In a design with four samples μ_1 and μ_4 will always be called different if $H_0: \mu_1 = ... = \mu_4$ is rejected. Now suppose that S_2^2 and s_3^2 are much smaler than s_1^2 and s_4^2. Then the difference between μ_1 and μ_4 may not be significant in a pairwise comparison. Here the structural difference between this test and generalisations of the multiple range test to unequal sample sizes and variance heterogeneity comes into the picture: If extreme means coincide with big variances or small samples, then these generalisations of the multiple range test can ignore important differences, while the Multiple James test can wrongly declare means to be different.

One can of course apply Welch's test for the Behrens-Fisher problem to the pairs that seem significant as a consequence of the Multiple James test. But if many pairwise comparisons are needed, and if for every pair the same level α is used, it is clear that we can loose control over the familywise error rate. So another strategy is needed and the answer is given by Einot and Gabriel (1975). If a multiple F-test is to be performed and the design is unbalanced one can simply start with the overall F-test with level α. If the hypothesis is rejected one does not look at the ordered sample means and try only the hypotheses $\mu_1 = ... = \mu_{k-1}$ and $\mu_2 = ... = \mu_k$, but every subset has to be considered where one μ_i is left out. The same values $\alpha_p^{D^*}$, α_p^R or α_p^W can be used with p = k-1 and the acceptance of a hypothesis means that the splitting process for this subset stops. This strategy is not limited to the second stage, but it is applied to every subset that becomes a candidate. For every step the level is some α_p where p is the number of samples in the subset under consideration. This approach will avoid the classical trap in the multiple F-test, but if it is applied to the multiple James test it can also handle the specific problem that comes from variance heterogeneity.

This strategy can be very expensive in computer-time. In the worst case situation, where all the means are isolated, the number of tests will be $2^k - (k+1)$ instead of only $\frac{1}{2} k(k-1)$ for the ordinary multiple James test or any strategy based on pairwise comparisons. For 15 samples this means 32752 tests instead of only 105. In order to find out whether this improved method is worth the additional computations, the ordinary multiple James test and this method were applied to 7 case studies with unbalanced designs and variance heterogeneity (from a chemical experiment and from a study on perception). There were 277 pairs and only for two of these the conclusions were different, meaning that the improved method did not confirm a pairwise significance that was found by the multiple James test.

The conclusion of this section can be that if one favours the multiple F-test one can deal with variance heterogeneity by modifying it into a multiple James test. The best choice for the level in every range under consideration is α_p^W by Welsch. If the improved strategy is too expensive in computer time, a terminal-oriented program should not only produce the final result, but also the separate sample sizes and standard deviations. If an interesting pairwise significance is based on samples where the sample sizes or standard deviations are very different, the user should confirm the outcome by using Welch's test for the Behrens-Fisher problem. The program should incorporate this possibility in a user-friendly conversation.

The results of a multiple James test can be represented by a vertical ordering of identified sample means with bars representing the possibly overlapping groups. This is visually more attractive than the matrix one needs for pairwise comparisons, especialy if there are many samples.

6.6. An example with unequal variances

Some of the methods mentioned in the previous sections will be applied to an example with four samples. The sample sizes are equal, but the variances are very different. The data are artificial; they are chosen in order to demonstrate the differences between some strategies. Table 3 gives the original data and table 4 is a summary of the relevant statistics.

Table 3: Four samples, $n_i = 15$			
1	2	3	4
-0.79	0.80	1.16	0.87
0.78	1.45	1.24	-1.02
-1.09	0.56	1.59	2.22
1.67	0.95	1.12	-0.03
2.26	0.88	1.51	2.11
1.57	0.52	1.21	3.93
0.55	0.82	1.44	2.95
-2.45	0.10	1.51	2.61
2.01	0.63	1.29	-0.63
0.58	0.86	0.90	0.96
2.27	0.56	1.88	3.39
0.58	1.05	1.78	2.31
1.36	0.82	0.98	4.99
4.63	0.24	1.40	1.65
-3.06	1.14	1.35	3.66

The variances of samples number 1 and 4 by far exceed those of number 2 and 3. The first stage of the multiple range test involves only the extreme samples and since they are already ordered this means that only the bigger variances are involved. Not assuming variance homogeneity the statistic will be based on the separately

Table 4: Summary of table 3			
sample	μ_i	σ_i	size
1	0.725	1.958	15
2	0.759	0.343	15
3	1.358	0.273	15
4	1.999	1.722	15

estimated variances with Welch's number of degrees of freedom. This results in 1.892 as the test statistic. The critical value here is $q_{4,28}/\sqrt{2}$ = 2.730 with level α = 0.05 so that the first hypothesis is accepted and the splitting process stops. Samples number 2 and 3 will therefore not be compared. And that is very unfortunate because the test statistic would be 7.478 with 27 degrees of freedom, resulting in an extremely significant difference.

The multiple James test (based on the ordered means) with level α = 0.05 results in two disjunct groups: samples 1 and 2 in one group and samples 3 an 4 in the other. Therefore the difference between μ_2 and μ_3 is recognized, but also some other pairwise differences that are not so convincing. In table 5 the results of the multiple James test are compared with the tail probability of Welch's test for every pair.

Table 5: Results of multiple James test		
pair	multiple James	Welch
1,2	accepted	0.948
1,3	rejected	0.234
1,4	rejected	0.069
2,3	rejected	0.000
2,4	rejected	0.015
3,4	accepted	0.175

The multiple James test rejects the equality of μ_1 and μ_4 with level α = 0.05 while a pairwise comparison leads to a tail probability of 0.069. This pseudo-paradox is a consequence of the strategy with ordered means. This strategy is only really appropriate if the sample sizes and variances are almost equal. An even more striking conflict can be seen by comparing the results for samples number 1 and 3.

The third approach that we will consider is based on pairwise comparisons. Ury & Wiggins, Tamhane and Games & Howell all use essentially the same test statistic; only the critical value is different (if there are more than two groups). In every case the number of degrees of freedom ν_{ij} comes from Welch's approximate solution for the Behrens-Fisher problem. The results are given in table 6.

pair	statistic	ν_{ij}
1,2	-0.066	15
1,3	-1.239	15
1,4	-1.892	28
2,3	-5.288	27
2,4	-2.736	15
3,4	-1.424	15

Table 6: Pairwise comparisons

The critical values for the tests under consideration are:

Ury & Wiggins: $t_{\nu_{ij}}(\beta/2)$ with $\beta = \dfrac{2\alpha}{k(k-1)}$

Tamhane: $t_{\nu_{ij}}(\gamma/2)$ with $\gamma = 1-(1-\alpha)^{\frac{2}{k(k-1)}}$

Games & Howell: $Q_{k,\nu_{ij}}(\alpha)/\sqrt{2}$

For four groups and the values of ν_{ij} that come from table 6 this results in critical values that are given in table 7. From tables 6 and 7 it is clear that the procedures by Ury & Wiggins, Tamhane and Games & Howell result in the same conclusions: Only the equality of μ_2 and μ_3 has to be rejected and the difference between μ_2 and μ_4 is almost significant.

This example demonstrates the dangers of using strategies based on ordered sample means in situations with variance heterogeneity. The

Table 7: Critical values (k = 4)			
ν_{ij}	Ury	Tamhane	Games
15	3.036	3.026	2.882
27	2.847	2.838	2.737
28	2.839	2.830	2.730

data were artificial; they were chosen specially in order to give as much discredit to these strategies as possible. It is clear that in this situation the methods based on pairwise comparisons result in the most acceptable conclusions.

6.7. Dealing with outliers

Just like in the previous chapter we will consider here contaminated normal data. With (small) probability ϵ the variance will be $a\sigma^2$ for some $a \gg 1$ and with probability $1-\epsilon$ the variance will remain σ^2. We saw that Huber's method performs very well in this situation with respect to power and control over the chosen size if one is interested in testing the overall hypothesis $\mu_1 = ... = \mu_k$. The method can be used to estimate the separate location parameters and it is also suitable for the within-groups variance. Therefore one can consider a modification of the multiple range test if the sample sizes are (almost) equal. A Multiple Huber test is also possible in this situation by using the F-statistic instead of the q-statistic. But if one permits the sample sizes to be unequal it is better to consider pairwise comparisons. Two tests will be examined. If the model does not permit outliers they are based on the following critical differences for the sample means:

Sidak: $t_{\nu}(\gamma/2)s \sqrt{1/n_i + 1/n_j}$ with $\gamma = 1 - (1-\alpha)^{\frac{2}{k(k-1)}}$

Kramer: $q_{k,\nu}(\alpha)s \sqrt{(1/n_i + 1/n_j)/2}$

If outliers are allowed ν can remain the same $N-k$, but the separate location parameters and s need modified estimators. We choose the estimators that are given in the previous chapter (see Huber's method) where the influence of the outliers is reduced considerably. The resulting tests will be denoted as Huber-Sidak and Huber-Kramer respectively. If there are no outliers we know already that the original Sidak and Kramer approaches are both conservative considering the familywise error rate. And we also know that Huber's test is slightly progressive, almost independently of the presence of outliers. In a simulation study we will try to find out whether this combination of conservatism and progressiveness will result in an acceptable control over the chosen size in the Huber-Sidak or Huber-Kramer test.

Table 8: Pairwise comparisons (Huber)				
n_i	ϵ	Kramer k=3	Sidak k=3	Kramer k=6	Sidak k=6
10	0	6.00	4.95	6.55	4.90
10	0.03	5.55	4.85	5.85	4.55
10	0.1	5.90	5.05	5.95	4.55
25	0	5.60	5.00	5.50	4.55
25	0.03	5.55	4.75	5.70	4.30
25	0.1	5.30	4.70	5.65	4.65
40	0	5.15	4.80	6.05	4.35
40	0.03	5.65	5.15	4.45	3.70
40	0.1	5.35	4.35	4.45	3.35
A	0	5.20	4.50	5.00	3.85
A	0.03	4.50	3.95	4.85	4.00
A	0.1	5.40	4.95	3.65	3.05

The entries in table 8 are based on 2000 replications each. The actual size is estimated by the percentage of rejected hypotheses. The nominal size is 5%, so that the standard error for these entries is given by $\sqrt{0.05 * 0.95/2000} = 0.00487$ or 0.487%. A fraction ϵ of the data were generated from a normal distribution with $\mu = 0$ and $\sigma^2 = 50$, and the remaining $1-\epsilon$ came from the standard normal distribution. The sample size A denotes [10,25,40] for three samples and [10,10,25,25,40,40] for six samples. From table 8 we can conclude that both tests give the user a reasonable amount of control over the chosen size. We knew already that the Kramer modification results in a uniformly more powerful test than pairwise t-tests with Sidak's γ. Since Huber's original test is a bit progressive it is not amazing that for three samples Huber-Sidak controls the chosen size better than Huber-Kramer. But all simultaneous tests based on pairwise comparisons tend to conservatism if the number of samples increases and the design is unbalanced. The simulation confirms this. Therefore Huber-Kramer is a better choice if there are many samples with unequal sample sizes.

6.8. An example with one outlier

Table 9: Six samples, $n_i = 10$					
1	2	3	4	5	6
1.68	1.71	1.91	1.91	1.85	2.03
1.66	1.68	1.74	1.89	1.84	2.00
1.66	1.67	1.72	1.85	1.84	1.95
1.59	1.64	1.68	1.84	1.82	1.92
1.57	1.62	1.68	1.83	1.79	1.92
1.56	1.61	1.68	1.79	1.79	1.91
1.56	1.61	1.65	1.77	1.78	1.90
1.55	1.59	1.61	1.76	1.77	1.89
1.52	1.56	1.58	1.74	1.74	1.89
1.46	1.53	1.53	1.70	1.72	1.77

Consider six samples from normal populations with ten observations each. The data are given in table 9. A summary of these data is given in table 10. Assuming variance homogeneity we may test $H_0: \mu_1 = \ldots = \mu_6$ by classical one-way analysis of means. The overall mean is 1.7335 and the pooled variance is 0.004974. The test statistic F is 32.98 with 5 degrees of freedom for the numerator and 54 for the denominator. The critical value here is 2.37 with level $\alpha = 0.05$. Therefore the hypothesis can be rejected. If we proceed with Hayter's modified Least Significant Difference test the critical value for the difference between two sample means is 0.0890. And if we ignore the

Table 10: Summary of table 9			
sample	mean	variance	sigma
1	1.581	0.00474	0.0689
2	1.622	0.00304	0.0551
3	1.678	0.01071	0.1035
4	1.808	0.00453	0.0673
5	1.794	0.00192	0.0438
6	1.918	0.00491	0.0700

information that the overall hypothesis has already been rejected we can use Tukey's method for pairwise comparisons yielding a critical value of 0.0932 for the same difference. In both cases 12 pairs are significantly different out of the total of 15. The differences of the sample means are given in table 11. We can use this strategy here because the sample sizes are equal.

Table 11: Differences of means					
sample	1	2	3	4	5
2	0.041				
3	0.097	0.056			
4	0.227	0.186	0.130		
5	0.213	0.172	0.116	0.014	
6	0.337	0.296	0.240	0.110	0.124

If we use Huber's method we get the following estimates for the location parameters: 1.584, 1.622, 1.670, 1.808, 1.794 and 1.922. The jointly estimated location parameter is 1.7333 and the residual variance is 0.004765. The test statistic is 35.16 with the same parameters as with classical anova and therefore also this method results in rejecting the hypothesis that all the populations have equal means. The differences of the robust estimates of the means are given in table 12. If we modify Hayter's Least Significant Difference test with Huber's estimates we get a critical value of 0.0871 for the differences between

Table 12: Differences of robust means					
sample	1	2	3	4	5
2	0.039				
3	0.085	0.047			
4	0.224	0.186	0.139		
5	0.210	0.171	0.125	0.014	
6	0.339	0.300	0.253	0.114	0.128

the estimated location parameters. Ignoring the fact that the overall hypothesis was rejected we can use Huber-Kramer or Huber-Sidak with critical values 0.0912 and 0.0946 respectively. Whatever we do, in all these cases 11 out of the 15 pairs differ significantly. The classical method found 12 differences and that is not very strange because for normal populations with equal variances the classical method yields the most powerful test.

Now suppose that the data represent heights of people from six groups. The data are given in meters, but the analyst (working at a terminal) has once forgotten to enter the decimal point. The last observation in the first group is the one where the mistake occured and so we have 146 instead of 1.46. The mean in the first group becomes 16.035, the sample variance 2085.29938 and the standard deviation 45.6651. This has considerable effect on the overall mean and the pooled variance; they become 4.1425 and 347.55408 respectively. Classical one-way anova results in $F = 0.97$ and that is far from being significant. Therefore we can not consider to proceed with the second stage of the Least Significant Difference test.

If we do not start with an overall test we can use Tukey's method for pairwise comparisons. But this test uses the pooled variance and therefore the influence of the outlier will also in this situation be considerable. The critical value for the sample means is 24.6309. The pairwise differences are given in table 13. From table 13 we can see that according to Tukey's classical test none of the pairwise comparisons results in a significant difference. Applying Huber's method here results in a

Table 13: Differences of means One extreme outlier					
sample	1	2	3	4	5
2	14.413				
3	14.357	0.056			
4	14.227	0.186	0.130		
5	14.241	0.172	0.116	0.014	
6	14.117	0.296	0.240	0.110	0.124

Table 14: Differences of robust means One extreme outlier					
sample	1	2	3	4	5
2	0.019				
3	0.065	0.047			
4	0.204	0.186	0.139		
5	0.190	0.171	0.125	0.014	
6	0.319	0.300	0.253	0.114	0.128

considerable improvement. The test statistic for H_0: $\mu_1 = \ldots = \mu_6$ is 32.36 so that this hypothesis can be rejected. The robust mean for the first group becomes 1.604; the other robust means are unaffected by the outlier. The jointly estimated location parameter is 1.7366 and the residual variance is 0.004828. Please note that these values differ only slightly from the ones obtained by Huber's method for the original data without the outlier. Using Huber's estimates in the next stage of Hayter's Least Significant Difference test results in critical value of 0.0877. If we ignore the result of the overall test we can use Huber-Kramer or Huber-Sidak with critical values 0.0918 and 0.0952 respectively. All these approaches result in the same conclusion: 11 pairs are significantly different (see table 14) and they are the same pairs that were found by these methods when there was no outlier.

6.9. Multiple range and multiple F tests with Huber's estimates

Ramsey (1978) demonstrated that the multiple range test and the multiple F test have more power (if the design is balanced) than any test based on pairwise comparisons. In the example with one outlier every group contained the same number of observations. Therefore we can use these tests here after modifying them to deal with outliers. The modification consists of using Huber's estimates for the location parameters and the residual variance. The resulting methods will be called multiple q^H test and multiple F^H test. First we will examine the multiple F test. Table 15 gives the critical F values as a function of the number of means in the range under consideration. The overall size $\alpha = 0.05$ and for every range with p means α_p^W by Welsch is used.

Table 15: Critical F values	
means	F value
2	6.072
3	3.938
4	3.115
5	2.543
6	2.386

For the samples without the outlier the results for the multiple F test are consistent with those for Hayter's modified Least Significant Difference test. They are presented in table 16.

Table 16: Differences of means					
sample	1	2	3	4	5
2	accept				
3	reject	accept			
4	reject	reject	reject		
5	reject	reject	reject	accept	
6	reject	reject	reject	reject	reject

If the outlier enters the data the multiple F test will not recognize any difference because the splitting process stops after the first stage. The multiple F^H test yields the same results for the data with and without the outlier. They are presented in table 17. If there is no outlier the multiple F test recognizes the difference between the first and the third

Table 17: Differences of robust means					
sample	1	2	3	4	5
2	accept				
3	accept	accept			
4	reject	reject	reject		
5	reject	reject	reject	accept	
6	reject	reject	reject	reject	reject

sample while the multiple F^H test fails to do so. But it is clear that the multiple F^H test is to be preferred if there is reason to suspect the presence of some extreme outliers.

The critical range in the multiple range test and the multiple q^H test depends on the estimated residual variance. Table 18 gives the critical values if the nominal size $\alpha = 0.05$ and if for the ranges under consideration α_p^W is chosen.

Table 18: Critical ranges				
means	S=0.0705	S=18.643	S=0.0690	S=0.0695
2	0.0777	20.544	0.0755	0.0766
3	0.0848	22.424	0.0830	0.0836
4	0.0887	23.444	0.0868	0.0874
5	0.0890	23.528	0.0871	0.0877
6	0.0932	24.632	0.0912	0.0918

Table 19: Summary of F and q tests			
statistic	method	outlier	differences
F	classical	no	12
F	classical	yes	0
F	robust	no	11
F	robust	yes	11
q	classical	no	12
q	classical	yes	0
q	robust	no	12
q	robust	yes	12

In table 18 the values of S (the square root of the residual variance) correspond from left to right with: (1) multiple range test, no outlier (2) multiple range test, one extreme outlier (3) multiple q^H test, no outlier and (4) multiple q^H test, one extreme outlier. The multiple range test recognizes all 12 differences if there is no outlier, but if the outlier is present the strategy stops after the first stage and no difference is found. The multiple q^H test also finds these 12 differences, but the outcome remains the same if the outlier is present. A summary of all the results mentioned in this section is given in table 19. This example suggests that the multiple q^H test has more power than the multiple F^H test. But that is highly unlikely because Ramsey (1978) has shown that in almost every situation the multiple F test is more powerful than the multiple range test (if the same α_p is used) but that the difference in power is very small. And there seems to be no reason why the order should be reversed if the classical estimates are replaced by Huber's alternatives.

The conclusion of this and the previous section can be the following: Classical methods for multiple comparisons are not robust against the presence of outliers. Even one single outlier can remove all power. And not only in an overall test, but also in pairwise comparisons if one uses the pooled variance. A modification of the classical methods using Huber's estimates for the location parameters and the residual variance results in a considerable improvement. The loss of power if there are no outliers is only marginal.

7. Appendices

7.1. The generation of random normal deviates

In this study pseudo-random normal deviates were generated using the method of Box and Muller (1958). Let U_1 and U_2 be independent random variables from the same rectangular density function on the interval $[0, 1)$. Using these one can generate a pair of random deviates from the same normal distribution as follows:

$$X_1 = \sqrt{-2\log_e U_1}\cos 2\pi U_2$$

$$X_2 = \sqrt{-2\log_e U_1}\sin 2\pi U_2$$

X_1 and X_2 will be independent normal variables with zero mean and unit variance as can be demonstrated by inverting the relationships:

$$U_1 = \exp\frac{-(X_1^2 + X_2^2)}{2}$$

$$U_2 = -\frac{1}{2\pi}\arctan\frac{X_2}{X_1}$$

This results in the joint density of X_1 and X_2:

$$f(X_1, X_2) = \frac{1}{2\pi}\exp\frac{-(X_1^2 + X_2^2)}{2} =$$

$$\frac{1}{\sqrt{2\pi}}\exp\frac{-X_1^2}{2} \cdot \frac{1}{\sqrt{2\pi}}\exp\frac{-X_2^2}{2} = f(X_1)f(X_2)$$

The pseudo-random real numbers U_1 and U_2 from the uniform distribution on the interval $[0, 1)$ were generated by the mixed congruential method. Let N be an integer starting-value. A new value for this variable is computed as:

$$N := (A*N + 116177073375)MOD\, 2^{39}$$

Where $A = 152587890725$ and $:=$ denotes the replacement operator. With this formula sequences of pseudo-random integers are generated. To get the desired real numbers the integers are divided by 2^{39}.

7.2. Computation of the F-distribution

The real function $FISPRO(x,n,d)$ computes the probability that an F-distributed variate does not exceed x. The number of degrees of freedom are n for the numerator and d for the denominator. This function is given by:

$$FISPRO(x,n,d) = C \int_0^x t^{\frac{1}{2}(n-2)}(d+tn)^{-\frac{1}{2}(n+d)}dt$$

Here x is a non-negative real and n and d are positive integers. The constant C is given as:

$$C = \frac{\Gamma((n+d)/2)}{\Gamma(\frac{1}{2}n)\Gamma(\frac{1}{2}d)} n^{\frac{1}{2}n} d^{\frac{1}{2}d}$$

A distinction is made between the following cases:

a. n + d ⩽ 500, n even.

$$Q = u^{\frac{1}{2}d}[1+\frac{1}{2}d(1-u)+\frac{d(d+2)}{2.4}(1-u)^2+ \ldots$$

$$+\frac{d(d+2)\ldots(d+n-4)}{2.4\ldots(n-2)}(1-u)^{\frac{1}{2}(n-2)}]$$

Here $u = d(d+nx)^{-1}$. The desired probability is then computed as FISPRO = 1 - Q. If Q happens to be negative then FISPRO = 1. This is also true for the following cases.

b. n + d ⩽ 500, d even.

$$Q = 1-(1-u)^{\frac{1}{2}n}[1+\frac{n}{2}u+\frac{n(n+2)}{2.4}u^2+ \ldots$$

$$+\frac{n(n+2)\ldots(n+d-4)}{2.4\ldots(d-2)}u^{\frac{1}{2}(d-2)}]$$

c. n + d ⩽ 500, n and d both odd. Let $\theta = \arctan\sqrt{nx/d}$. Then Q = 1 - A + β, where A and β are given as follows: If d = 1 then A = $2\theta/\pi$. If d ⩾ 2, then:

$$A = \frac{2}{\pi}[\theta + \sin\theta + 2\cos^3\theta/3 + \ldots + \frac{2.4 \ldots (d-3)}{3.5 \ldots (d-2)}\cos^{d-2}\theta]$$

If n = 1 then β = 0. If n ⩾ 2 then:

$$\beta = \frac{2}{\sqrt{\pi}} \frac{((d-1)/2)!}{((d-2)/2)!}\sin\theta \cos^d \theta [1 + \frac{d+1}{3}\sin^2\theta + \ldots$$

$$+ \frac{(d+1)(d+3) \ldots (d+n-4)}{3.5 \ldots (n-2)}\sin^{n-3}\theta]$$

d.   n + d > 500, 10d ⩽ n. Q is computed as if the variate were χ^2-distributed. The procedure CHIPRO is called with d degrees of freedom, and the argument is given as:

$$v = \frac{1 + \dfrac{d-1}{2n}}{\dfrac{1}{xd} + \dfrac{1}{2n}}$$

e.   n + d > 500, 10 n ⩽ d. Q is computed by CHIPRO with n degrees of freedom and argument:

$$v = \frac{1 + \dfrac{n-1}{2d}}{\dfrac{1}{xn} + \dfrac{1}{2d}}$$

In all other cases:

$$Q = \frac{1}{2} ERF(\frac{-\sqrt{2}(1-f_2)f_3/2 + f_1 - 1}{\sqrt{f_2 f_3^2 + f_1}}) + \frac{1}{2}$$

Here $f_1 = \frac{2}{9n}$, $f_2 = \frac{2}{9d}$ and $f_3 = x^{\frac{1}{3}}$. ERF denotes the error function that is defined as follows:

$$ERF(x) = \frac{2}{\sqrt{\pi}} \int_0^x \exp(-t^2)dt$$

For this function a very stable algorithm is used that yields an accuracy of at least 10 digits. In this study only the cases a, b and c are encountered. The precision here is 10^{-6}.

Lackritz (1984) gave a more attractive method for finding the p-value of an F-test. Unfortunately, this method came to the attention of the present author when the simulation study was finished already.

7.3. Computation of the inverse χ^2 distribution

A real function $CHISTA(\alpha,\nu,\epsilon)$ is defined as follows: The tail probability of a χ^2-distributed variate with ν degrees of freedom is α. The value for which this probability is reached is computed with precision ϵ and the result is stored in CHISTA. The algorithm consists of two parts:

a. The estimation of a reasonable initial estimate x_0 of the solution x. Here we use the abbreviation $p = 1-\alpha$. If $\nu=1$, then $\sqrt{x_0}$ is computed by the inverse standard normal probability function $NOSTAT$ with parameter $1-(p+1)/2$ and precision ϵ. If $\nu=2$, then $x_0 = -2\log_e(1-p)$. If $\nu > 2$, then:

$$x_0 = \nu(1-\frac{2}{9n}+t\ \sqrt{2*(9n)^{-1}})^3$$

Where t is computed by the inverse standard normal probability function with tail probability α. If $\nu=1$ or $\nu=2$ then $x = x_0$ and the desired value has been found. If:

$$p < \frac{0.35^{\frac{n}{2}}}{n\ 2^{\frac{n}{2}}\Gamma(\frac{n}{2})}$$

or if in the last case the initial estimate is negative, then we use x_0^1 instead of x_0, where:

$$x_0^1 = (2^{\frac{n}{2}}\Gamma(\frac{n}{2}+1)p)^{\frac{2}{n}}$$

b. The second part of the algorithm is an iteration with Newton's method until the precision ϵ has been reached. The starting value is x_0 or x_0^1:

$$x_{i+1} = x_i - \frac{CHIPRO(x_i) - p}{f(x_i)}$$

Here the procedure CHIPRO computes the χ^2-distribution with ν degrees of freedom. The derivative $f(x_i)$ is given as follows:

$$f(x_i) = \frac{x_i^{\frac{1}{2}n-1} e^{-\frac{1}{2}x_i}}{2^{\frac{n}{2}} \Gamma(\frac{n}{2})}$$

During this process negative values of x_{i+1} can occur. In this case a Regula Falsi is used instead of Newton's method. In this study the precision ϵ has been given the value 10^{-4}.

Now a description of the function CHIPRO for the χ^2-distribution wil be given. The result will be the tail probability α that is defined by:

$$\alpha = \frac{1}{2^m \Gamma(m)} \int_x^\infty t^{m-1} e^{-\frac{1}{2}t} dt$$

Here m = $\nu/2$. The computation of this probability is based on the following recurrent relation:

$$\alpha(\nu) = \alpha(\nu-2) + (\frac{x}{2})^{m-1} \frac{\exp(-\frac{x}{2})}{\Gamma(m)}$$

A distinction is made between two cases:

1. ν is even; n = 2m.

$$\alpha(\nu) = \exp(-\frac{x}{2}) \sum_{i=2}^{m} (\frac{x}{2})^{i-1} \frac{1}{\Gamma(i)} + \alpha(2)$$

Here $\alpha(2)$ is computed as $\exp(-\frac{x}{2})$.

2. ν is odd; n = $2m_1 + 1$.

$$\alpha(\nu) = \exp(-\frac{x}{2}) \sum_{i=2}^{m_1} (\frac{x}{2})^{i-\frac{1}{2}} \frac{1}{\Gamma(i+\frac{1}{2})} + \alpha(1)$$

$$\alpha(1)= \frac{2}{\sqrt{2\pi}} \int\limits_{w}^{\infty} \exp(-\tfrac{1}{2} t^2)dt$$

Here $w = \sqrt{x}$.

Now we only have to explain the computation of the inverse standard normal distribution function. The algorithm consists of two parts:

a. The computation of a reasonable initial estimate x_0 of x:

$$x_0= (t - \frac{c_0+c_1t +c_2t^2}{1+d_1t +d_2t^2+d_3t^3})sgn$$

Here $t = \sqrt{\log_e (p^{-2})}$ and sgn = 1 if $0 < p \leqslant 0.5$. If $0.5 < p < 1$ then sgn = -1 and $t = \sqrt{\log_e ([1-p]^{-2})}$. NOSTAT will be given the value 6 if p = 1 and -6 if p = -1. The constants in the function for the initial estimate are:

c_0 = 2.515517
c_1 = 0.802853
c_2 = 0.010328
d_1 = 1.432788
d_2 = 0.189269
d_3 = 0.001308

b. Iteration with Newton's method until a precision ϵ has been reached. The starting value is x_0:

$$x_{i+1}= x_i - \frac{NOPROB(x_i)-p}{f(x_i)}$$

$$f(x_i)= \frac{1}{\sqrt{2\pi}} \exp(-\tfrac{1}{2} x_i^2)$$

Here NOPROB gives the standard normal distribution function:

$$NOPROB(x)= \frac{1}{\sqrt{2\pi}} \int\limits_{-\infty}^{x} \exp(-\tfrac{1}{2} t^2)dt$$

For this function a very stable algorithm is used that is accurate to at least 10 digits.

7.4. The generation of double exponential, logistic and Cauchy variates

The density of the double exponential distribution (also known as the laplace distribution) is:

$$F(x) = \frac{1}{2\sigma} \exp\left(-\frac{|x-\mu|}{\sigma}\right)$$

Here x is a real number, μ and σ are the parameters to be chosen by the user with the restriction that σ has to be positive. Random numbers from this distribution are generated as follows. At first a random number u is drawn from the open interval $(0,1)$. Then y is a random variate from the double exponential distribution if:

$$y = \mu + \sigma \log_e (2u) \text{ for } u \leqslant \tfrac{1}{2}$$

$$y = \mu - \sigma \log_e (2(1-u)) \text{ for } \tfrac{1}{2} < u$$

This transformation was mentioned by Van Putten and Van der Tweel (1979).

The logistic distribution has the following cumulative distribution function:

$$F(x) = \frac{1}{1 + \exp\left(-\frac{x-\alpha}{\beta}\right)}$$

Here x is a real number, α and β are the parameters than can be chosen by the user. The scale parameter β has to be positive. Let u be a uniform random number from the open interval $(0,1)$. Then a random number y from the logistic distribution can be got from the transformation:

$$y = \alpha - \beta \log_e \left(\frac{1-u}{u}\right)$$

This tranformation has been given by Newman and Odell (1971).

The density of the Cauchy distribution is given by:

$$f(x) = \frac{1}{\sigma \pi} \frac{1}{1 + (\frac{x-\mu}{\sigma})^2}$$

Again x is a real number, μ and σ can be chosen by the user and σ has to be positive. Let u be a uniform random number from the open interval (0,1). The following transformation will result in a random number y from the cauchy distribution:

$$y = \mu + \sigma \tan((u - \tfrac{1}{2})\pi)$$

This transformation was mentioned by Van Putten and Van der Tweel (1979).

7.5. The limiting values of Q for some distributions

In this section the values of the statistic Q for the uniform, normal, logistic, double exponential and Cauchy distribution as the sample size tends to infinity will be derived. This statistic is defined as follows:

$$Q = \frac{10(U_{.05} - L_{.05})}{U_{.5} - L_{.5}}$$

Here $U_{.05}$ denotes the sum of the upper 5% of the observations. If the sample size is not a multiple of 20 then one observation is only fractionally included. The other parts of this formula have a similar meaning where L stands for lower. For symmetrical distributions Q can be given as follows (for infinite sample sizes):

$$Q = \frac{10 \int\limits_{c}^{\infty} x f(x) dx}{\int\limits_{0}^{\infty} x f(x) dx}$$

Here c is the upper 5% point of the distribution F with density f. For the uniform distribution we take the range from $-\tfrac{1}{2}$ to $\tfrac{1}{2}$ with density $f(x) = 1$. So we have:

$$Q_U = \frac{10 \int_{.45}^{.5} x\,dx}{\int_0^{.5} x\,dx} = 1.9$$

For the standard normal distribution the value of c is 1.645. So Q can be computed here as follows:

$$Q_N = \frac{10 \frac{1}{\sqrt{2\pi}} \int_{1.645}^{\infty} x e^{-\frac{1}{2}x^2}\,dx}{\frac{1}{\sqrt{2\pi}} \int_0^{\infty} x e^{-\frac{1}{2}x^2}\,dx} = 10 e^{-\frac{1}{2}1.645^2} = 2.58$$

For the logistic distribution we take the simplest form where $F(x) = (1+e^{-x})^{-1}$ and therefore $c = \log_e 19$. This results in:

$$Q_L = \frac{10 \int_c^{\infty} \frac{x e^{-x}}{(1+e^{-x})^2}\,dx}{\int_0^{\infty} \frac{x e^{-x}}{(1+e^{-x})^2}\,dx}$$

$$\int_c^{\infty} \frac{x e^{-x}}{(1+e^{-x})^2}\,dx =$$

$$c\left(1 - \frac{1}{1+e^{-c}}\right) + \int_c^{\infty} \frac{e^{-x}}{1+e^{-x}}\,dx =$$

$$\frac{c e^{-c}}{1+e^{-c}} + \log_e(1+e^{-c})$$

$$Q_L = 10 \frac{\frac{\log_e 19}{20} + \log_e\left(\frac{20}{19}\right)}{\log_e 2} = 2.86$$

For the double exponential distribution we take the standard form and look at the density of the absolute values, so that the left tail is mirrored in the axis of symmetry. We have:

$$\int_0^\infty xe^{-x} = 1$$

In the numerator we use $c = \log_e 10$ because then $1 - e^{-c} = 0.90$. This results in the following value for Q:

$$Q_D = 10 \int_{\log_e 10}^\infty xe^{-x}\, dx = 10(\log_e 10 + 1)e^{-\log_e 10} = 3.30$$

For the Cauchy distribution the value of Q is given by:

$$Q_C = \lim_{d \to \infty} \frac{10 \int_c^d \dfrac{x}{1+x^2}dx}{\int_0^d \dfrac{x}{1+x^2}dx} = \lim_{d \to \infty} \frac{10(\log_e (1+d^2) - \log_e (1+c^2))}{\log_e (1+d^2)} = 10$$

And this result is independent of the value of c. For the adaptive tests it would be more attractive to have a formula for the expectation of the modus or the median for finite samples of given size. This problem seems very difficult and it has not yet been solved.

8. Literature

Abramowitz, M. and I.A. Stegun (1964) Handbook of mathematical functions.
Washington D.C. National Bureau of Standards. 940-943.

Andrews, F.C. (1954) Asymptotic behaviour of some rank tests for analysis of variance.
The Annals of Mathematical Statistics (25) 724-736.

Banerjee, S.K. (1961) On confidence intervals for two-means problem based on separate estimates of variances and tabulated values of t-variable.
Sankhya (A23).

Beaton, A.E. and J.W. Tukey (1974) The fitting of power series, meaning polynomials, illustrated on band-spectroscopic data.
Technometrics (16) 147-185.

Box, G.E.P. and M.E. Muller (1958) A note on the generation of random normal deviates.
The Annals of Mathematical Statistics (29) 610-611.

Bradley, J.V. (1968) Distribution-free statistical tests.
Prentice-Hall. Englewood Cliffs.

Brown, G.W. and A.M. Mood (1950) On median tests for linear hypotheses.
Proceedings of the second Berkeley Symposium. 159-166.

Brown, M.B. and A.B. Forsythe (1974) The small sample behaviour of some statistics which test the equality of several means.
Technometrics (16) 129-132.

Dijkstra, J.B. and P.S.P.J. Werter (1981) Testing the equality of several means when the population variances are unequal.
Communications in Statistics. Simulation and Computation (B10-6) 557-569.

Dijkstra, J.B. and P.S.P.J. Werter (1982) Het gebruik van de toets van Kruskal en Wallis bij normale verdelingen met ongelijke varianties.
Kwantitatieve Methoden (5) 151-158.

Dijkstra, J.B. (1984) Nonparametric comparison of several mean values with mild adaptation to some sample characteristics.
COMPSTAT Conference. Prague.

Dijkstra, J.B. (1983) Robustness of multiple comparisons against variance heterogeneity.
Robustness of Statistical Methods and Nonparametric Statistics. Proceedings of a Conference at Schwerin (GDR) 18-22.

Dijkstra, J.B. (1986) Robuuste variantie-analyse.
Eindhoven University of Technology. Computing Centre Note 30.
Statistische Dag VVS. Tilburg.

Dijkstra, J.B. and H. Linders (1987) Comparison of severall mean
values in the presence of outliers.
Kwantitatieve Methoden (25).

Dixon, W.J. and J.W. Tukey (1968) Approximate behaviour of the distribution of winsorized t.
Technometrics (10) 83-98.

Duncan D.B. (1951) A significance test for differences between ranked
treatments in an analysis of variances.
Virginia Journal of Science (2).

Duncan, D.B. (1955) Multiple range and multiple F-tests.
Biometrics (11) 1-42.

Duncan, D.B. (1952) On the properties of the multiple comparisons
test.
Virginia Journal of Science (3).

Einot, I and K.R. Gabriel (1975) A study of the powers of several
methods of multiple comparisons.
Journal of the Americal Statistical Association (70) 574-583.

Ekbohm, G. (1976) On testing the equality of several means with
small samples.
The Agricultural College of Sweden (Uppsala) 547-553.

Fisher, R.A. (1935) The design of experiments.
Oliver and Boyd. Edinburgh and London.

Fung, K.Y. and S.M. Rahman (1980) The two-sample winsorized t.
Communications in Statistics (B 9-4) 337-347.

Games, P.A. and J.F. Howell (1976) Pairwise multiple comparison procedures with unequal N's and/or variances: a monte carlo study.
Journal of Educational Statistics (1) 113-125.

Games, P.A., H.J. Keselma and J.C. Rogan (1983) A review of simultaneous pairwise multiple comparisons.
Statistica Neerlandica (37) 53-58.

Hajek, J. (1969) A course in nonparametric statistics.
Holden-Day. San Francisco.

Hajek, J. and Z. Sidak (1967) Theory of rank tests.
Academia (Prague).

Hampel, F.R., E.M. Ronchetti, P.J. Rousseeuw and W.A. Stahel (1986)
Robust statistics: The approach based on influence functions.

John Wiley & Sons, New York.

Hayter, A.J. (1984) A proof of the conjecture that the Tukey-Kramer multiple comparisons procedure is conservative.
The Annals of Statistics (12) 61-75.

Hayter, A.J. (1986) The maximum familywise error rate of Fisher's Least Significant Difference test.
Journal of the American Statistical Association (81) 1000-1004.

Hochberg, Y (1976) A modification of the T-method of multiple comparisons for a one-way lay-out with unequal variances.
Journal of the American Statistical Association (71) 200-203.

Hodges, J.L. and E.L. Lehmann (1961) Comparison of the normal scores and Wilcoxon tests.
Proceedings of the Fourth Berkeley Symposium on Mathematical Statistics and Probability. University of California Press (1) 307-317.

Hogg, R.V. (1974) Adaptive robust procedures: A partial review and some suggestions for future applications and theory.
Journal of the American Statistical Association (69) 909-923.

Hogg, R.V., D.M. Fisher and R.H. Randles (1975) A two-sample adaptive distribution-free test.
Journal of the American Statistical Association (70) 656-661.

Holland, P.W. and R.E. Welsh (1977) Robust regression using iteratively reweighted least-squares.
Communications in Statistics (A 6-9) 813-827.

Huber, P.J. (1972) Robust statistics: a review.
The Annals of Mathematical Statistics (43) 1041-1067.

Huber, P.J. (1973) Robust regression: asymptotics, conjectures and Monte Carlo.
Annals of Statistics (1) 799-821.

Huber, P.J. (1981) Robust statistics.
John Wiley and Sons. New York.

Iman, R.L., D. Quade and D.A. Alexander (1975) Exact probabiblity levels for the Kruskal-Wallis test.
Selected Tables in Mathematical Statistics. American Mathematical Scociety. Volume III.

James, G.S. (1951) The comparison of several groups of observations when the ratios of the population variances are unknown.
Biometrika (38) 324-329.

Keuls, M. (1952) The use of the studentized range in connection with an analysis of variance.
Euphytica (1) 112-122.

Kramer, C.Y. (1956) Extension of multiple range tests to group means with unequal numbers of replications.
Biometrics (12) 307-310.

Kroon, J. de and P. van der Laan (1981) Distribution-free test procedures in two-way layouts; a concept of rank-interaction.
Statistica Neerlandica (35, no 4) 189-213.

Kruskal, W.H. and W.A. Wallis (1952) Use of ranks in one-criterion variance analysis.
Journal of the American Statistical Association (47) 583-621. See also (1953: 48) 907-911.

Laan, P. van der and J. Oosterhoff (1967) Experimental determination of the power functions of the two-sample rank tests of Wilcoxon, Van der Waerden and Terry by Monte Carlo techniques.
Statistica Neerlandica (21, no 1) 55-68.

Lackritz, J.R. (1984) Exact p-values for F and t tests.
The American Statistician (38) 312-314.

Leroy, A. and P. Rousseeuw (1985) A multiple regression technique for detecting outliers.
Kwantitatieve Methoden (6, no 8) 41-58.

Ludwig, O.C. (1962) Algorithm 179, the incomplete beta ratio.
Collected Algorithms from CACM.

Miller, R.G. (1966) Simultaneous statistical inference.
McGraw-Hill Book Company. New York.

Mood, A.M., F.A. Graybill and D.C. Boes (1963) Introduction to the theory of statistics.
McGraw-Hill Series in Probability and Statistics.

Newman, D. (1939) The distribution of the range in samples from a normal population, expressed in terms of an independent estimate of standard deviation.
Biometrika (31) 20-30.

Newman, T.G. and P.L. Odell (1971) The generation of random variates.
Griffin. London.

Peiser, A.M. (1943) Asymptotic formulas for significance levels of certain distributions.
Annals of Mathematical Statistics (14) 56-62.

Peiser, A.M. (1949) Correction to "Asymptotic formulas for significance levels of certain distributions".
Annals of Mathematical Statistics (20) 128-129.

Petrinovich, L.F. and C.D. Hardyck (1969) Error rates for multiple comparison methods: some evidence concerning the frequency of erroneous conclusions.
Psychological Bulletin (71) 43-54.

Pike, M.C. and I.D. Hill (1963) Remark on algorithm 179, the incomplete beta ratio.
Communications of the ACM.

Puri, M.L. (1964) Asymptotic efficiency of a class of c-sample tests.
Annals of Mathematical Statistics (35) 102-121.

Putten, C. van and I. van der Tweel (1979) On generating random variables.
Mathematisch Centrum. Amsterdam.

Ramsey, P.H. (1978) Power differences between pairwise multiple comparisons.
Journal of the American Statistical Association (73) 479-485.

Ramseyer, G.C. and T. Tcheng (1973) The robustness of the studentized range statistic to violations of the normality and homogeneity of variance assumptions.
American Educational Research Journal (10).

Rousseeuw, P.J. (1984) Least median of squares regression.
Journal of the American Statistical Association (79) 871-880.

Rousseeuw, P.J. and A.M. Leroy (1987) Robust regression and outlier detection.
John Wiley and Sons, New York.

Ryan, T.A. (1960) Significance tests for multiple comparison of proportions, variances and other statistics.
Psychological Bulletin (57) 318-328.

Satterthwaite, F.E. (1941) Synthesis of variance.
Psychometrika (6) 309-316.

Scheffé, H. (1944). A note on the Behrens-Fisher problem.
The Annals of Mathematical Statistics (15) 430-432.

Scheffé, H. (1943) On solutions of the Behrens-Fisher problem, based on the t-distribution.
The Annals of Mathematical Statistics (14) 35-44.

Scheffé, H. (1970) Practical solutions of the Behrens-Fisher problem.
Journal of the American Statistical Association (65, no 332)

1501-1508.

Sen, P.K. (1962) On studentized non-parametric multi-sample location tests.
Annals of the Institute of Statistical Mathematics (14) 119-131.

Sidak, Z. (1967) Rectangular confidence regions for the means of multivariate normal distributions.
American Statistical Association Journal (62) 626-633.

Tamhane, A.C. (1977) Multiple comparisons in model-1 one-way anova with unequal variances.
Communications in Statistics (A 6-1) 15-32.

Tamhane, A.C. (1979) A comparison of procedures for multiple comparisons of means with unequal variances.
Journal of the American Statistical Association (74) 471-480.

Terry, M.E. (1960) An optimum replicated two-sample test using ranks.
Contributions to Probability and Statistics. Stanford University Press. 444-447.

Tukey, J.W. (1979) Study of robustness by simulation: particularly improvement by adjustment and combination.
In: Robustness in Statistics (edited by R.L. Launer and G.N. Wilkinson) Academic Press.

Ury, H.K. and A.D. Wiggins (1971) Large sample and other multiple comparisons among means.
British Journal of Mathematical and Statistical Psychology (24) 174-194.

Uthoff, V.A. (1973) The most powerful scale and location invariant test of the normal versus the double exponential.
The Annals of Statistics (1) 170-174.

Uthoff, V.A. (1970) An optimum test property of two well-known statistics.
Journal of the American Statistical Association (65) 1597-1600.

Waerden, B.L. van der (1952) Order tests for the two-sample problem and their power.
Indagationes Math. (14) 453-458.

Wallace, D.L. (1959) Simplified Beta-approximations to the Kruskal-Wallis H-test.
Journal of the American Statistical Association (54) 225-230.

Wallace, D.L. (1980) The Behrens-Fisher and Fieller-Creasy problems.
In: R.A. Fisher: An Appreciation (edited by S.E. Fienberg and D.V. Hinkley) Springer-Verlag.

Wang, Y.Y. (1971) Probabilities of type I errors of the Welch tests for the Behrens-Fisher problem.
Journal of the American Statistical Association (66) 605-608.

Welch, B.L. (1938) The significance of the difference between two means when the population variances are unequal.
Biometrika (29) 350-362.

Welch, B.L. (1949) Further note on Mrs. Aspin's tables and on certain approximations to the tabled function.
Biometrika (36) 293-296.

Welch, B.L. (1951) On the comparison of several mean values: an alternative approach.
Biometrika (38) 330-336.

Welch, B.L. (1947) The generalization of Student's problem when several different population variances are involved.
Biometrika (34) 28-35.

Welsch, R.E. (1977) Stepwise multiple comparison procedures.
Journal of the American Statistical Association (72) 566-575.

Winer, B.J. (1962) Statistical principles in experimental design.
McGraw-Hill. New York.

Yuen, K.K. and W.J. Dixon (1973) The approximate behaviour and performance of the two-sample trimmed t.
Biometrika (60) 369-374.

9. Subject index

10. Short summary

This tract is about the hypothesis that a number of location parameters are equal. Unequal sample sizes are allowed and for the error distribution various models are considered. For some methods the distribution of the test statistic under the hypothesis is only approximately known. In those cases a validation of the method is based on simulations for a representative collection of values for the population parameters.

For normally distributed errors variance heterogeneity is allowed. It is demonstrated that in this situation the method of James with a second order Taylor approximation for the critical value is superior to some more recent methods, considering the control over the chosen level. The power of this test is not uniformly dominated by any other existing alternative, and therefore it is recommended as the best choice.

Some statisticians use the Kruskal and Wallis test for the hypothesis of equal means in all situations where the classical test for one-way analysis of means can not be applied. It is shown that this is not to be recommended if the scale parameters are unequal. At least if one uses the exact distribution of the test statistic or the well known χ^2 approximation. A limited amount of variance heterogeneity can be handled by the Beta approximation of Wallace, but the price one has to pay here is a (sometimes considerable) loss of power.

If the only thing that is known about the error distribution is the fact that it is symmetric, an adaptive nonparametric test can be considered that uses optimal scores for the estimated tail-weight. It is demonstrated that such a test has more power than any of the existing nonparametric tests for the hypothesis of equal means, if the error distribution is a mixture with equal occurences of the following densities: uniform, normal, logistic, double exponential and Cauchy.

The power of the classical method for one-way analysis of means can be completely removed by one single outlier. Some more robust alternatives will be considered: trimming, Winsorizing, Van der Waerden's test, Huber's proposal, Least Median of Squares (Rousseeuw) and an adaptive nonparametric test. A simulation is perfomed for symmetric and one-sided contamination. It is shown that Huber's proposal results in the most powerful test with satisfactory control over the chosen level.

For the problem of Multiple Comparisons in the classical situation with normal populations and variance homogeneity the following strategies are well known: Least Significant Difference test (Fisher), pairwise comparisons based on the t-distribution, Multiple Range tests (Newman, Duncan and Keuls), Multiple F-tests (Duncan) and Tukey's Wholly Significant Difference test. Modifications of these methods to situations with variance heterogeneity or to the presence of some extreme outliers are examined.

MATHEMATICAL CENTRE TRACTS

1 T. van der Walt. *Fixed and almost fixed points.* 1963.

2 A.R. Bloemena. *Sampling from a graph.* 1964.

3 G. de Leve. *Generalized Markovian decision processes, part I: model and method.* 1964.

4 G. de Leve. *Generalized Markovian decision processes, part II: probabilistic background.* 1964.

5 G. de Leve, H.C. Tijms, P.J. Weeda. *Generalized Markovian decision processes, applications.* 1970.

6 M.A. Maurice. *Compact ordered spaces.* 1964.

7 W.R. van Zwet. *Convex transformations of random variables.* 1964.

8 J.A. Zonneveld. *Automatic numerical integration.* 1964.

9 P.C. Baayen. *Universal morphisms.* 1964.

10 E.M. de Jager. *Applications of distributions in mathematical physics.* 1964.

11 A.B. Paalman-de Miranda. *Topological semigroups.* 1964.

12 J.A.Th.M. van Berckel, H. Brandt Corstius, R.J. Mokken, A. van Wijngaarden. *Formal properties of newspaper Dutch.* 1965.

13 H.A. Lauwerier. *Asymptotic expansions.* 1966, out of print; replaced by MCT 54.

14 H.A. Lauwerier. *Calculus of variations in mathematical physics.* 1966.

15 R. Doornbos. *Slippage tests.* 1966.

16 J.W. de Bakker. *Formal definition of programming languages with an application to the definition of ALGOL 60.* 1967.

17 R.P. van de Riet. *Formula manipulation in ALGOL 60, part 1.* 1968.

18 R.P. van de Riet. *Formula manipulation in ALGOL 60, part 2.* 1968.

19 J. van der Slot. *Some properties related to compactness.* 1968.

20 P.J. van der Houwen. *Finite difference methods for solving partial differential equations.* 1968.

21 E. Wattel. *The compactness operator in set theory and topology.* 1968.

22 T.J. Dekker. *ALGOL 60 procedures in numerical algebra, part 1.* 1968.

23 T.J. Dekker, W. Hoffmann. *ALGOL 60 procedures in numerical algebra, part 2.* 1968.

24 J.W. de Bakker. *Recursive procedures.* 1971.

25 E.R. Paërl. *Representations of the Lorentz group and projective geometry.* 1969.

26 European Meeting 1968. *Selected statistical papers, part I.* 1968.

27 European Meeting 1968. *Selected statistical papers, part II.* 1968.

28 J. Oosterhoff. *Combination of one-sided statistical tests.* 1969.

29 J. Verhoeff. *Error detecting decimal codes.* 1969.

30 H. Brandt Corstius. *Exercises in computational linguistics.* 1970.

31 W. Molenaar. *Approximations to the Poisson, binomial and hypergeometric distribution functions.* 1970.

32 L. de Haan. *On regular variation and its application to the weak convergence of sample extremes.* 1970.

33 F.W. Steutel. *Preservation of infinite divisibility under mixing and related topics.* 1970.

34 I. Juhász, A. Verbeek, N.S. Kroonenberg. *Cardinal functions in topology.* 1971.

35 M.H. van Emden. *An analysis of complexity.* 1971.

36 J. Grasman. *On the birth of boundary layers.* 1971.

37 J.W. de Bakker, G.A. Blaauw, A.J.W. Duijvestijn, E.W. Dijkstra, P.J. van der Houwen, G.A.M. Kamsteeg-Kemper, F.E.J. Kruseman Aretz, W.L. van der Poel, J.P. Schaap-Kruseman, M.V. Wilkes, G. Zoutendijk. *MC-25 Informatica Symposium.* 1971.

38 W.A. Verloren van Themaat. *Automatic analysis of Dutch compound words.* 1971.

39 H. Bavinck. *Jacobi series and approximation.* 1972.

40 H.C. Tijms. *Analysis of (s,S) inventory models.* 1972.

41 A. Verbeek. *Superextensions of topological spaces.* 1972.

42 W. Vervaat. *Success epochs in Bernoulli trials (with applications in number theory).* 1972.

43 F.H. Ruymgaart. *Asymptotic theory of rank tests for independence.* 1973.

44 H. Bart. *Meromorphic operator valued functions.* 1973.

45 A.A. Balkema. *Monotone transformations and limit laws.* 1973.

46 R.P. van de Riet. *ABC ALGOL, a portable language for formula manipulation systems, part 1: the language.* 1973.

47 R.P. van de Riet. *ABC ALGOL, a portable language for formula manipulation systems, part 2: the compiler.* 1973.

48 F.E.J. Kruseman Aretz, P.J.W. ten Hagen, H.L. Oudshoorn. *An ALGOL 60 compiler in ALGOL 60, text of the MC-compiler for the EL-X8.* 1973.

49 H. Kok. *Connected orderable spaces.* 1974.

50 A. van Wijngaarden, B.J. Mailloux, J.E.L. Peck, C.H.A. Koster, M. Sintzoff, C.H. Lindsey, L.G.L.T. Meertens, R.G. Fisker (eds.). *Revised report on the algorithmic language ALGOL 68.* 1976.

51 A. Hordijk. *Dynamic programming and Markov potential theory.* 1974.

52 P.C. Baayen (ed.). *Topological structures.* 1974.

53 M.J. Faber. *Metrizability in generalized ordered spaces.* 1974.

54 H.A. Lauwerier. *Asymptotic analysis, part 1.* 1974.

55 M. Hall, Jr., J.H. van Lint (eds.). *Combinatorics, part 1: theory of designs, finite geometry and coding theory.* 1974.

56 M. Hall, Jr., J.H. van Lint (eds.). *Combinatorics, part 2: graph theory, foundations, partitions and combinatorial geometry.* 1974.

57 M. Hall, Jr., J.H. van Lint (eds.). *Combinatorics, part 3: combinatorial group theory.* 1974.

58 W. Albers. *Asymptotic expansions and the deficiency concept in statistics.* 1975.

59 J.L. Mijnheer. *Sample path properties of stable processes.* 1975.

60 F. Göbel. *Queueing models involving buffers.* 1975.

63 J.W. de Bakker (ed.). *Foundations of computer science.* 1975.

64 W.J. de Schipper. *Symmetric closed categories.* 1975.

65 J. de Vries. *Topological transformation groups, 1: a categorical approach.* 1975.

66 H.G.J. Pijls. *Logically convex algebras in spectral theory and eigenfunction expansions.* 1976.

68 P.P.N. de Groen. *Singularly perturbed differential operators of second order.* 1976.

69 J.K. Lenstra. *Sequencing by enumerative methods.* 1977.

70 W.P. de Roever, Jr. *Recursive program schemes: semantics and proof theory.* 1976.

71 J.A.E.E. van Nunen. *Contracting Markov decision processes.* 1976.

72 J.K.M. Jansen. *Simple periodic and non-periodic Lamé functions and their applications in the theory of conical waveguides.* 1977.

73 D.M.R. Leivant. *Absoluteness of intuitionistic logic.* 1979.

74 H.J.J. te Riele. *A theoretical and computational study of generalized aliquot sequences.* 1976.

75 A.E. Brouwer. *Treelike spaces and related connected topological spaces.* 1977.

76 M. Rem. *Associons and the closure statement.* 1976.

77 W.C.M. Kallenberg. *Asymptotic optimality of likelihood ratio tests in exponential families.* 1978.

78 E. de Jonge, A.C.M. van Rooij. *Introduction to Riesz spaces.* 1977.

79 M.C.A. van Zuijlen. *Empirical distributions and rank statistics.* 1977.

80 P.W. Hemker. *A numerical study of stiff two-point boundary problems.* 1977.

81 K.R. Apt, J.W. de Bakker (eds.). *Foundations of computer science II, part 1.* 1976.

82 K.R. Apt, J.W. de Bakker (eds.). *Foundations of computer science II, part 2.* 1976.

83 L.S. van Benthem Jutting. *Checking Landau's "Grundlagen" in the AUTOMATH system.* 1979.

84 H.L.L. Busard. *The translation of the elements of Euclid from the Arabic into Latin by Hermann of Carinthia (?), books vii-xii.* 1977.

85 J. van Mill. *Supercompactness and Wallman spaces.* 1977.

86 S.G. van der Meulen, M. Veldhorst. *Torrix I, a programming system for operations on vectors and matrices over arbitrary fields and of variable size.* 1978.

88 A. Schrijver. *Matroids and linking systems.* 1977.

89 J.W. de Roever. *Complex Fourier transformation and analytic functionals with unbounded carriers.* 1978.

90 L.P.J. Groenewegen. *Characterization of optimal strategies in dynamic games.* 1981.

91 J.M. Geysel. *Transcendence in fields of positive characteristic.* 1979.

92 P.J. Weeda. *Finite generalized Markov programming.* 1979.

93 H.C. Tijms, J. Wessels (eds.). *Markov decision theory.* 1977.

94 A. Bijlsma. *Simultaneous approximations in transcendental number theory.* 1978.

95 K.M. van Hee. *Bayesian control of Markov chains.* 1978.

96 P.M.B. Vitányi. *Lindenmayer systems: structure, languages, and growth functions.* 1980.

97 A. Federgruen. *Markovian control problems; functional equations and algorithms.* 1984.

98 R. Geel. *Singular perturbations of hyperbolic type.* 1978.

99 J.K. Lenstra, A.H.G. Rinnooy Kan, P. van Emde Boas (eds.). *Interfaces between computer science and operations research.* 1978.

100 P.C. Baayen, D. van Dulst, J. Oosterhoff (eds.). *Proceedings bicentennial congress of the Wiskundig Genootschap, part I.* 1979.

101 P.C. Baayen, D. van Dulst, J. Oosterhoff (eds.). *Proceedings bicentennial congress of the Wiskundig Genootschap, part 2.* 1979.

102 D. van Dulst. *Reflexive and superreflexive Banach spaces.* 1978.

103 K. van Harn. *Classifying infinitely divisible distributions by functional equations.* 1978.

104 J.M. van Wouwe. *Go-spaces and generalizations of metrizability.* 1979.

105 R. Helmers. *Edgeworth expansions for linear combinations of order statistics.* 1982.

106 A. Schrijver (ed.). *Packing and covering in combinatorics.* 1979.

107 C. den Heijer. *The numerical solution of nonlinear operator equations by imbedding methods.* 1979.

108 J.W. de Bakker, J. van Leeuwen (eds.). *Foundations of computer science III, part 1.* 1979.

109 J.W. de Bakker, J. van Leeuwen (eds.). *Foundations of computer science III, part 2.* 1979.

110 J.C. van Vliet. *ALGOL 68 transput, part I: historical review and discussion of the implementation model.* 1979.

111 J.C. van Vliet. *ALGOL 68 transput, part II: an implementation model.* 1979.

112 H.C.P. Berbee. *Random walks with stationary increments and renewal theory.* 1979.

113 T.A.B. Snijders. *Asymptotic optimality theory for testing problems with restricted alternatives.* 1979.

114 A.J.E.M. Janssen. *Application of the Wigner distribution to harmonic analysis of generalized stochastic processes.* 1979.

115 P.C. Baayen, J. van Mill (eds.). *Topological structures II, part 1.* 1979.

116 P.C. Baayen, J. van Mill (eds.). *Topological structures II, part 2.* 1979.

117 P.J.M. Kallenberg. *Branching processes with continuous state space.* 1979.

118 P. Groeneboom. *Large deviations and asymptotic efficiencies.* 1980.

119 F.J. Peters. *Sparse matrices and substructures, with a novel implementation of finite element algorithms.* 1980.

120 W.P.M. de Ruyter. *On the asymptotic analysis of large-scale ocean circulation.* 1980.

121 W.H. Haemers. *Eigenvalue techniques in design and graph theory.* 1980.

122 J.C.P. Bus. *Numerical solution of systems of nonlinear equations.* 1980.

123 I. Yuhász. *Cardinal functions in topology - ten years later.* 1980.

124 R.D. Gill. *Censoring and stochastic integrals.* 1980.

125 R. Eising. *2-D systems, an algebraic approach.* 1980.

126 G. van der Hoek. *Reduction methods in nonlinear programming.* 1980.

127 J.W. Klop. *Combinatory reduction systems.* 1980.

128 A.J.J. Talman. *Variable dimension fixed point algorithms and triangulations.* 1980.

129 G. van der Laan. *Simplicial fixed point algorithms.* 1980.

130 P.J.W. ten Hagen, T. Hagen, P. Klint, H. Noot, H.J. Sint, A.H. Veen. *ILP: intermediate language for pictures.* 1980.

131 R.J.R. Back. *Correctness preserving program refinements: proof theory and applications.* 1980.

132 H.M. Mulder. *The interval function of a graph.* 1980.

133 C.A.J. Klaassen. *Statistical performance of location estimators.* 1981.

134 J.C. van Vliet, H. Wupper (eds.). *Proceedings international conference on ALGOL 68.* 1981.

135 J.A.G. Groenendijk, T.M.V. Janssen, M.J.B. Stokhof (eds.). *Formal methods in the study of language, part I.* 1981.

136 J.A.G. Groenendijk, T.M.V. Janssen, M.J.B. Stokhof (eds.). *Formal methods in the study of language, part II.* 1981.

137 J. Telgen. *Redundancy and linear programs.* 1981.

138 H.A. Lauwerier. *Mathematical models of epidemics.* 1981.

139 J. van der Wal. *Stochastic dynamic programming, successive approximations and nearly optimal strategies for Markov decision processes and Markov games.* 1981.

140 J.H. van Geldrop. *A mathematical theory of pure exchange economies without the no-critical-point hypothesis.* 1981.

141 G.E. Welters. *Abel-Jacobi isogenies for certain types of Fano threefolds.* 1981.

142 H.R. Bennett, D.J. Lutzer (eds.). *Topology and order structures, part 1.* 1981.

143 J.M. Schumacher. *Dynamic feedback in finite- and infinite-dimensional linear systems.* 1981.

144 P. Eijgenraam. *The solution of initial value problems using interval arithmetic; formulation and analysis of an algorithm.* 1981.

145 A.J. Brentjes. *Multi-dimensional continued fraction algorithms.* 1981.

146 C.V.M. van der Mee. *Semigroup and factorization methods in transport theory.* 1981.

147 H.H. Tigelaar. *Identification and informative sample size.* 1982.

148 L.C.M. Kallenberg. *Linear programming and finite Markovian control problems.* 1983.

149 C.B. Huijsmans, M.A. Kaashoek, W.A.J. Luxemburg, W.K. Vietsch (eds.). *From A to Z, proceedings of a symposium in honour of A.C. Zaanen.* 1982.

150 M. Veldhorst. *An analysis of sparse matrix storage schemes.* 1982.

151 R.J.M.M. Does. *Higher order asymptotics for simple linear rank statistics.* 1982.

152 G.F. van der Hoeven. *Projections of lawless sequences.* 1982.

153 J.P.C. Blanc. *Application of the theory of boundary value problems in the analysis of a queueing model with paired services.* 1982.

154 H.W. Lenstra, Jr., R. Tijdeman (eds.). *Computational methods in number theory, part I.* 1982.

155 H.W. Lenstra, Jr., R. Tijdeman (eds.). *Computational methods in number theory, part II.* 1982.

156 P.M.G. Apers. *Query processing and data allocation in distributed database systems.* 1983.

157 H.A.W.M. Kneppers. *The covariant classification of two-dimensional smooth commutative formal groups over an algebraically closed field of positive characteristic.* 1983.

158 J.W. de Bakker, J. van Leeuwen (eds.). *Foundations of computer science IV, distributed systems, part 1.* 1983.

159 J.W. de Bakker, J. van Leeuwen (eds.). *Foundations of computer science IV, distributed systems, part 2.* 1983.

160 A. Rezus. *Abstract AUTOMATH.* 1983.

161 G.F. Helminck. *Eisenstein series on the metaplectic group, an algebraic approach.* 1983.

162 J.J. Dik. *Tests for preference.* 1983.

163 H. Schippers. *Multiple grid methods for equations of the second kind with applications in fluid mechanics.* 1983.

164 F.A. van der Duyn Schouten. *Markov decision processes with continuous time parameter.* 1983.

165 P.C.T. van der Hoeven. *On point processes.* 1983.

166 H.B.M. Jonkers. *Abstraction, specification and implementation techniques, with an application to garbage collection.* 1983.

167 W.H.M. Zijm. *Nonnegative matrices in dynamic programming.* 1983.

168 J.H. Evertse. *Upper bounds for the numbers of solutions of diophantine equations.* 1983.

169 H.R. Bennett, D.J. Lutzer (eds.). *Topology and order structures, part 2.* 1983.

CWI TRACTS

1 D.H.J. Epema. *Surfaces with canonical hyperplane sections.* 1984.

2 J.J. Dijkstra. *Fake topological Hilbert spaces and characterizations of dimension in terms of negligibility.* 1984.

3 A.J. van der Schaft. *System theoretic descriptions of physical systems.* 1984.

4 J. Koene. *Minimal cost flow in processing networks, a primal approach.* 1984.

5 B. Hoogenboom. *Intertwining functions on compact Lie groups.* 1984.

6 A.P.W. Böhm. *Dataflow computation.* 1984.

7 A. Blokhuis. *Few-distance sets.* 1984.

8 M.H. van Hoorn. *Algorithms and approximations for queueing systems.* 1984.

9 C.P.J. Koymans. *Models of the lambda calculus.* 1984.

10 C.G. van der Laan, N.M. Temme. *Calculation of special functions: the gamma function, the exponential integrals and error-like functions.* 1984.

11 N.M. van Dijk. *Controlled Markov processes; time-discretization.* 1984.

12 W.H. Hundsdorfer. *The numerical solution of nonlinear stiff initial value problems: an analysis of one step methods.* 1985.

13 D. Grune. *On the design of ALEPH.* 1985.

14 J.G.F. Thiemann. *Analytic spaces and dynamic programming: a measure theoretic approach.* 1985.

15 F.J. van der Linden. *Euclidean rings with two infinite primes.* 1985.

16 R.J.P. Groothuizen. *Mixed elliptic-hyperbolic partial differential operators: a case-study in Fourier integral operators.* 1985.

17 H.M.M. ten Eikelder. *Symmetries for dynamical and Hamiltonian systems.* 1985.

18 A.D.M. Kester. *Some large deviation results in statistics.* 1985.

19 T.M.V. Janssen. *Foundations and applications of Montague grammar, part 1: Philosophy, framework, computer science.* 1986.

20 B.F. Schriever. *Order dependence.* 1986.

21 D.P. van der Vecht. *Inequalities for stopped Brownian motion.* 1986.

22 J.C.S.P. van der Woude. *Topological dynamix.* 1986.

23 A.F. Monna. *Methods, concepts and ideas in mathematics: aspects of an evolution.* 1986.

24 J.C.M. Baeten. *Filters and ultrafilters over definable subsets of admissible ordinals.* 1986.

25 A.W.J. Kolen. *Tree network and planar rectilinear location theory.* 1986.

26 A.H. Veen. *The misconstrued semicolon: Reconciling imperative languages and dataflow machines.* 1986.

27 A.J.M. van Engelen. *Homogeneous zero-dimensional absolute Borel sets.* 1986.

28 T.M.V. Janssen. *Foundations and applications of Montague grammar, part 2: Applications to natural language.* 1986.

29 H.L. Trentelman. *Almost invariant subspaces and high gain feedback.* 1986.

30 A.G. de Kok. *Production-inventory control models: approximations and algorithms.* 1987.

31 E.E.M. van Berkum. *Optimal paired comparison designs for factorial experiments.* 1987.

32 J.H.J. Einmahl. *Multivariate empirical processes.* 1987.

33 O.J. Vrieze. *Stochastic games with finite state and action spaces.* 1987.

34 P.H.M. Kersten. *Infinitesimal symmetries: a computational approach.* 1987.

35 M.L. Eaton. *Lectures on topics in probability inequalities.* 1987.

36 A.H.P. van der Burgh, R.M.M. Mattheij (eds.). *Proceedings of the first international conference on industrial and applied mathematics (ICIAM 87).* 1987.

37 L. Stougie. *Design and analysis of algorithms for stochastic integer programming.* 1987.

38 J.B.G. Frenk. *On Banach algebras, renewal measures and regenerative processes.* 1987.

39 H.J.M. Peters, O.J. Vrieze (eds.). *Surveys in game theory and related topics.* 1987.

40 J.L. Geluk, L. de Haan. *Regular variation, extensions and Tauberian theorems.* 1987.

41 Sape J. Mullender (ed.). *The Amoeba distributed operating system: Selected papers 1984-1987.* 1987.

42 P.R.J. Asveld, A. Nijholt (eds.). *Essays on concepts, formalisms, and tools.* 1987.

43 H.L. Bodlaender. *Distributed computing: structure and complexity.* 1987.

44 A.W. van der Vaart. *Statistical estimation in large parameter spaces.* 1988.

45 S.A. van de Geer. *Regression analysis and empirical processes.* 1988.

46 S.P. Spekreijse. *Multigrid solution of the steady Euler equations.* 1988.

47 J.B. Dijkstra. *Analysis of means in some non-standard situations.* 1988.